party food for vegetarians

celia brooks brown

party food
for vegetarians

photography by Jan Baldwin

LAUREL
GLEN

San Diego, California

contents

foreword

"A vegetarian is not a person who lives on vegetables, any more than a Catholic is a person who lives on cats."—George Bernard Shaw

There are all sorts of reasons for giving up or cutting down on meat. For me, meat is something that has just never been appealing. I was nineteen when I moved to Britain from the U.S. in 1989, and back then I ate chicken occasionally, but I'd never eaten much other meat. I was no gourmet—I lived on canned soup, salads, and fast food. Boiling water and opening cans was the extent of my culinary skills. Not long after I arrived, there was a food scare in Britain. It put me off chicken, and I gave up meat for good.

Soon after giving up meat, I started to develop an interest in cooking. This is no coincidence. I knew I couldn't live on cans of beans and lumps of fatty cheese. As my mental perception of food became more acute—I started to see food as something other than just fuel—my sensory perception improved too. I was desperate to learn how to cook, so I could explore the creative process of using ingredients, tools, and all five senses to make something delicious. The greatest satisfaction of all, I found, was giving other people pleasure through eating what I prepared. I soon discovered that food that is cooked with passion evokes passion in the person eating it.

The whole realm of food is a healthy obsession for me, and it's not limited to cooking. So much of the fun and fascination lies in shopping for fresh, high-quality ingredients in specialty food stores. It also includes poring through books about food and filling my head with recipes, folklore, and culinary and social history. I'm also rather partial to stuffing my face.

My passion became a career in vegetarian cooking through catering, teaching, and writing. I'm certainly no vegetarian "evangelist." I merely hope to show people how easy and fun it can be to cook, and meat is simply not part of my repertoire. You must have what I call a "sensory relationship" with what you cook. If you can't engage every sense with your ingredients, what you cook just won't taste right. Even if I were to go through the mechanics of cooking a piece of meat, it would probably taste horrible.

My approach, in a nutshell, is this: Vegetarian cooking is more complex than simply throwing something under the broiler. It requires more thought, more construction. If you're not used to vegetarian cooking, try to think beyond the "meat and two vegetables" convention, in which vegetables play second fiddle. Try to create a balance of textures, colors, and flavors, and no one will notice the absence of meat.

Finally, when I tell people I'm vegetarian, the question that often follows is, "Do you eat fish?" OK, so vegetarians who eat fish are not technically vegetarians, but since when has the enjoyment of food been a technical business? I don't see it as hypocrisy to eat a bit of fish. People should be allowed to make their own decisions about what they put in their bodies and why. (That includes meat-eaters.) This modern breed of "pescetarians" are not rare, so I've included some fish recipes here for them, having done my best to recommend fish that is as eco-friendly as possible. This book is for every food lover, vegetarian or not. I hope you savor every page.

Celia Brooks Brown

how to use this book

—These days, what you decide to cook is as much determined by the event—a casual brunch party or perhaps a swanky cocktail dinner—as the time of year. So, I've grouped the recipes by the occasions they lend themselves to. At the beginning of each chapter is some advice and a few organizational tips, while in the middle I have suggested a menu for the occasion and given advice on planning, presentation, and drinks. All the recipes are designed for you to create a menu for everyone to enjoy, not just vegetarians, and I hope that some of the dishes will become part of your daily repertoire as well.

plan ahead—the golden rules of entertaining

Rule 1   **A strong menu is the foundation of success:**

Design a menu that's convenient to prepare in the time available.

Stick to seasonal ingredients.

Balance the color, flavor, and texture of every part of the meal.

Determine your budget—you can be generous without spending a fortune.

Think outside the appetizer-main-dessert box. Consider serving several small courses, or canapés followed by an extraordinary main course.

Consider the weather and how it affects what you want to eat—for example, cold soup on a hot day is magic.

Provide a little something to eat with alcoholic drinks, even if it's as simple as a bowl of nuts or olives.

Rule 2   **Make life easy for yourself wherever possible:**

Consider renting plates, cutlery, or even tables and chairs. Rental companies might even let you send everything back dirty for a small charge.

Consider your entertaining space—people inevitably gravitate to the kitchen at parties, but try to let the party actually happen well away from the working space.

Clean out your refrigerator—you can never have too much fridge space. Borrow space in your neighbor's fridge—as long as you invite them to the party! For a big event, rent a refrigerator.

Get your shopping out of the way the day before you start cooking.

Rope in as much human help as possible. Appoint or hire one helper for every ten guests.

If you've got lots of kids coming, provide a different menu for them, but don't knock yourself out cooking for them! Provide them with the stuff they'll like: chips, pizza, and sweets in individual packages as well as some of the simpler grown-up food.

If you are heating or cooking kids' food, don't forget to factor that in to oven and fridge space.

Rule 3
Remember the mundane but crucial details:

Get a big trash can ready. Buy plenty of garbage bags.

More and more people seem to have food intolerances these days. It is their responsibility to tell you ahead of time if they have special requirements. If they tell you once they've arrived and there's nothing for them to eat, don't feel bad—let them raid the kitchen.

Don't forget paper napkins—little ones for canapés, large ones for everything else, and at least two per person.

If it's cold outside, have a place where people can put their coats.

bar basics

If you're the cook, appoint someone else to be in charge of the bar.

Rough quantities of wine: Allow half a bottle of white wine and half a bottle of red wine per person. If you are serving champagne all night, allow three-fourths of a bottle per person.

If you can buy it "sale or return" from your wine merchant, opt for more.

Open nonsparkling wine and replace the corks before people arrive.

Save wine boxes for empty bottles. Recycle.

Consider renting glasses. Many liquor stores offer free glass rental, provided that you send them back clean. Some will inevitably break. For a big party, rent twice as many wineglasses as guests. People have one drink, put their glass down, then when they're ready for another, they forget where they put it or it's been cleared away, so they'll be needing another.

Provide tumblers as well as wineglasses for nonalcoholic drinks and cocktails.

Get one pillow-size bag of ice (about 25 lb. for every ten people).

Call an ice company that will deliver. Start chilling drinks at least two hours before the party.

Drinks chill faster in an ice bath (ice plus water) than on ice alone or in the fridge.

Don't clog your fridge with alcohol. Fill your bathtub with ice and water instead.

Provide lots of sparkling and plain mineral water.

For a big party, don't offer too many different drinks. Stick with wine and beer—or one fabulous cocktail.

Keep the nonalcoholic drinks simple. Provide a cordial such as elderflower or a pitcher of thawed concentrated juice for mixing with mineral water.

shopping & storage strategies

Make space in your fridge and in the kitchen for your ingredients before you shop.

Think quality. Buy the best of everything you can get.

If you come across a real bargain, you might consider altering the menu—but only if it's a fresh, high-quality ingredient. For instance, don't buy two-for-one strawberry cartons if they're looking past their best!

Organic food is usually superior, but it's more perishable. Inspect fresh produce carefully and use as soon as possible. Washed root vegetables will perish faster.

Organic eggs are always superior. Store in the fridge.

Ethnic food stores are treasure troves and can be an inspirational source of raw ingredients and special, unique desserts.

Support small businesses. Buy local produce whenever possible.

Salad greens and fresh herbs should be purchased no earlier than a day before your party.

Spray lettuce with water and store in the fridge, away from the fridge walls in order to avoid "fridge burn."

Bunches of fresh herbs should be washed and kept in a vase of water.

Never refrigerate basil or tomatoes. Keep berries in the fridge.

Take all fruit and vegetables out of any plastic packaging.

health matters

When you're entertaining, it's time to live a little. Indulgence is a good thing—in moderation. The fact is, healthy food makes you feel good—it boosts energy levels, strength, and vitality. On a day-to-day basis, everyone benefits from a healthy diet—that means low fat, lots of complex carbohydrates (like whole grains), fiber, a little protein, and plenty of fresh fruits and vegetables. I think the occasional naughty nibble is also essential for good spirits.

a vegetarian diet is a model diet

Research has shown that a vegetarian diet improves health, which is a great reason to eat vegetarian food on occasion or all the time. Vegetarians need to replace the nutrients that meat contains, in particular protein, iron, B vitamins, and selenium. Sources of these nutrients are abundant in an ideal vegetarian diet, which consists of a variety of foods including grains, beans, legumes, fruit, vegetables, nuts, seeds, and a small amount of fat. It's best not to rely on cheese as a source of protein—animal fat is saturated fat—although low-fat dairy products like yogurt are an important source of calcium. Eggs are packed with essential nutrients, but should also be eaten in moderation.

the entertainer's bag of tricks——Following is a list of useful ingredients to store in the kitchen so you're always prepared to cook with confidence, comfort, and finesse.

flavors for salty seasoning	**Soy sauce**—dark (fermented), light (unfermented) **Thai fish sauce**—nam pla **Worcestershire sauce**—traditional or vegetarian **Stock**—high-quality vegetable stock powder or cubes
flavors for heat and spice	**Chilies**—fresh (store in freezer indefinitely or fridge until crinkly), dried (smoked and nonsmoked), cayenne pepper, mild chili powder; chili sauces: Thai, sweet chili, Tabasco, Jamaican hot; pickled chilies (sliced jalapeños, whole varieties); smoked Spanish paprika (pimenton) **Whole spices**—black mustard seeds, pink peppercorns, fennel seeds, cumin seeds, coriander seeds, cardamom, fenugreek, saffron strands, whole nutmegs, cinnamon sticks, vanilla beans
flavors for depth, body, and accent	**Oils and vinegars**—extra-virgin olive oil; sesame, truffle, and walnut oils; aged balsamic and rice vinegars **Alcohol for cooking**—Madeira, sherry, vermouth (substitute for white wine), mirin (Japanese cooking wine), port, brandy or cognac, rum **Fresh herbs**—Italian parsley, basil, mint, sage, bay leaves, cilantro
flavors for a sweet tooth	Honey, pouring syrup, molasses, malt extract, rose water, orange blossom water, lemon curd Pure unsweetened cocoa, 70 percent cocoa solids, semisweet chocolate, white chocolate
tasty morsels	Assorted olives, capers in vinegar or salt, capers, sun-dried or semidried tomatoes in oil (semidried usually store in the fridge), artichoke hearts in oil, pickled onions, pickled baby beet, cornichons and pickled cucumbers, dried cèpes, dried shiitake mushrooms, canned stuffed vine leaves, canned hummus **Nuts**—(all shelled) pine nuts, peanuts, vacuum-packed chestnuts, hazelnuts, walnuts, pecans, pistachios, cashew nuts, almonds (whole blanched, slivered, ground), peanut butter **Seeds**—(all hulled) sesame seeds, poppy seeds, pumpkin seeds, hemp seeds **Dried fruits**—raisins, golden raisins, apricots, prunes, cranberries, figs, coconut
staples	**Noodles and pasta**—egg, rice, soba, and vermicelli noodles; linguine; pasta shapes; orzo pasta **Rice and other grains**—basmati, risotto, whole-grain, and long-grain rice; couscous; bulgur wheat; quinoa grains **Legumes and canned vegetables**—lentils, dried beans, canned beans of all sorts (including refried beans), artichoke hearts, roasted bell peppers, hearts of palm, roasted green chilies, water chestnuts
freezer essentials	Chopped and leaf spinach, peas, frozen berries, dough, ice cream, kaffir lime leaves, lemongrass, chilies, bread such as Turkish flatbread, tortillas, vodka, ice

1

canapés & cocktail bites

simple little bites with minimum fuss, to serve with drinks

Canapé is derived from a French word meaning "couch"—a tasty morsel reclining on an edible cushion before being popped in the mouth. The word has come to encompass all party nibbles—something tiny but delicious, to indulge the taste buds and buffer the effects of alcohol.

There's no doubt that hot, crispy nibbles are usually the most popular food to accompany drinks, but only if they're served as soon as they're cooked. This means that the cook is stuck in the kitchen and the grease is stuck to the cook (and the cook's fancy clothes). If you're still up for it, visit the freezer department of an Asian food store and you'll find tasty vegetarian spring rolls, dim sum, and wontons (read the labels to double-check for any hidden meat ingredients). Sink them into hot oil until golden, then serve with chili sauce.

If you're the cook and the host, however, rely on your best friend, the oven, to do the cooking while you see to other things. It's a good idea to carry a small kitchen timer with you if you leave things in the oven while the guests arrive. The smell of burned food is distinctive and embarrassing. Believe me, I've done it more than once.

The selection of canapés you choose should be a logical balance of hot and cold, and low on last-minute labor. Here are my guidelines on quantity (per guest):

Before-lunch canapés: 2–3 different canapés, 1–2 of each
As an appetizer: 3 different canapés, 1–2 of each
Early evening cocktail party: 6–8 different canapés, 1–2 of each
Canapés in place of an evening meal: 8 different canapés, 2–3 of each
Stick to the smaller quantity when providing canapés that are larger than one bite.

cucumber & herbed mascarpone bites

Here, the quintessentially English cucumber sandwich gets dressed up in a modern style and nibbled out of a carved bread bowl. Make up to four hours in advance.

ingredients

makes 36

1 large, round, rustic loaf of bread

9 oz. mascarpone cheese

4 heaping tablespoons finely chopped fresh herbs, such as dill, parsley, tarragon, and chives

grated zest of 1 lemon

salt and freshly ground black pepper

2–3 shakes Tabasco sauce

8 slices whole-wheat sandwich bread

1/2 cucumber, sliced paper-thin

method

To make the container, cut a circle out of the top of the loaf, leaving a border around the edge. Hollow out to form a "bread bowl," then cover with plastic wrap until ready to use.

Beat together the mascarpone cheese, herbs, lemon zest, salt, pepper, and Tabasco sauce, then spread evenly over two slices of bread. Place a layer of cucumber slices over the mixture on one slice, then top with the other slice of bread. Slice off the crusts, then cut each sandwich into nine little squares. Repeat with the remaining ingredients.

Fill the bread bowl with the sandwich bites, cover with plastic wrap, and keep in the refrigerator until ready to serve. (You may have enough bites to refill the bowl.)

spice-crusted baby potatoes with tamarind cream

These tiny potatoes, studded with crunchy spices, are always a treat. The dip has an element of surprise—the tamarind—that really gets people talking. Cherry-sized potatoes are ideal, as they can just be popped in the mouth.

ingredients

serves 20 as part of a canapé menu, 8–10 as finger food

2 lb. 4 oz. baby new potatoes, scrubbed

1 tablespoon coriander seeds

1 tablespoon cumin seeds

1/2 teaspoon ground turmeric

1/2 teaspoon cayenne pepper

1 teaspoon celery salt or sea salt

3 tablespoons olive oil

1 tablespoon wine vinegar

for the tamarind cream:

scant 1/2 cup crème fraîche or sour cream

scant 1/2 cup plain yogurt

2 tablespoons prepared tamarind, diluted to drizzling consistency if thick (see Top Tip below)

method

Preheat the oven to 425°F. Boil the potatoes in enough well-salted water to cover for 5 minutes, then drain and let cool. Dry them with a clean cloth.

Grind the coriander and cumin seeds in a mortar or spice grinder, then mix with the remaining spices and salt. Whisk together the oil, vinegar, and spices in a bowl. Place the potatoes in a large roasting pan, then pour the oil mixture on top and toss well to coat evenly. Roast them in the oven for about 15–20 minutes, until tender. Use tongs to remove the potatoes from the roasting pan and set aside until required. Reserve the toasted spices left in the pan.

For the tamarind cream, beat together the crème fraîche or sour cream and yogurt, then stir in the reserved spices. Scrape the cream mixture into a bowl and drizzle the tamarind on top. Serve with warm or cold potatoes. Use toothpicks if desired.

top tip

To prepare tamarind from pulp, briefly soak a hunk in boiling water, then press through a strainer (see photos above).

cranberry phyllo cigars

Sweet and sour cranberries combined with almonds, capers, and spice give these crispy nibbles an intriguing flavor. Is it sweet or is it savory? People have fun trying to guess just what goes into these Middle Eastern–inspired pastries.

ingredients

makes about 15

1/2 cup dried cranberries

1/2 cup ground almonds

1 tablespoon capers in vinegar, drained

1 tablespoon fresh oregano or marjoram, leaves stripped

1/2 teaspoon cumin seeds

4 small sheets phyllo pastry (approximately 6 1/4 x 12 in.)

2 tablespoons butter, melted

method

Preheat the oven to 425°F. Place the cranberries in a bowl and add enough boiling water to cover. Let soak for 15–20 minutes or until soft, then drain thoroughly. Place the reconstituted cranberries, ground almonds, capers, oregano or marjoram, and cumin seeds in a food processor or spice grinder and process until a purée results. Alternatively, chop everything very small and combine thoroughly.

Lightly grease a cookie sheet and line with parchment paper. Lay a sheet of phyllo pastry out horizontally on a clean, flat surface and brush all over with melted butter. Keep the rest of the pastry sheets covered with a damp towel. Along the bottom of the pastry, about 3/4 in. above the edge, arrange a long strip of the filling, about a pencil's width. Fold the bottom edge carefully over the filling, then roll the entire long sausage up tightly, moving along in sections, until rolled into a long cigar.

Using a knife or kitchen scissors, snip off the very ends of the cigar, then snip into baby cigars about 2 in. long. Place on the cookie sheet and brush generously with butter. Repeat with the remaining pastry.

Bake the cigars in the preheated oven for about 10–15 minutes, until golden all over. Serve warm or cold.

think ahead

Make the cigars up to the stage before cutting and baking a day in advance. Keep in the refrigerator, covered and not touching each other.

top tip

Vegans can use olive oil in place of butter. When serving, these cigars have a habit of sliding around on the plate, so they're best served on a bamboo mat or from a bowl.

eggplant, feta, & mint skewers

Charbroiled eggplants look great dressed in black stripes—but you could oven-broil them instead. Assemble the skewers up to four hours in advance.

ingredients

makes 20

1 long, thin eggplant, sliced as thinly as possible lengthwise into ten slices

olive oil, for brushing

3 1/2 oz. feta cheese, cut into approximately 3/4 in. cubes

20 large, fresh mint leaves

freshly ground black pepper

pomegranate molasses (page 71) or vintage balsamic vinegar, for drizzling

method

Place a ridged grill pan over high heat for 5 minutes or until very hot. Brush the eggplant slices with olive oil, then charbroil on both sides until translucent and striped with black. Let cool, then cut each slice into two long strips. Take one strip at a time and place a mint leaf on top, then tightly wrap both around a piece of feta. Secure with a bamboo skewer or cocktail stick and place on a large serving plate. Season to taste with black pepper, then drizzle with a little pomegranate molasses or a few drops of balsamic vinegar.

eggplant, feta, & mint skewers (left), cranberry phyllo cigars (right)

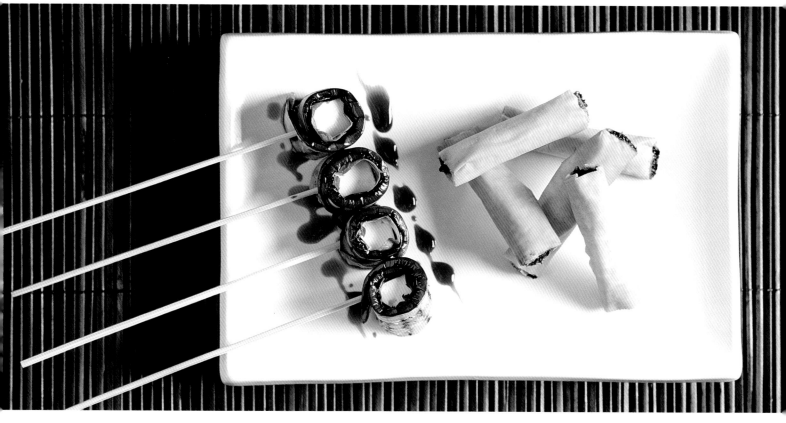

serving cocktails

Cocktail parties have a lively energy—people are usually standing around, talking, so they often drink more quickly than usual. Consequently, it's important to keep the food flowing as well as the drinks, but try to pace it over the evening. If you're busy in the kitchen, nominate friends or family members to circulate with your creations, explaining exactly what's in each one in case the guests ask. Don't fuss around with too many garnishes—let the food speak for itself. Keep each canapé small, tidy, and bite size. Provide receptacles for used cocktail sticks, olive pits, empty shot glasses, etc., and don't send hot food out too hot.

shopping	Asian food stores are always worth a visit for party paraphernalia like toothpicks, funky napkins, serving dishes and glasses, candles, nuts, and nibbles.
presentation	For serving canapés use plates, bowls, lacquer trays, and bamboo steamer baskets. Assemble canapés on kitchen trays, then transfer to the serving dishes. Don't put too many canapés on at once: nobody ever wants the last, lone canapé.
drinks	The best way to get a party going is for the host to serve one strong cocktail to everyone as they arrive. Try: **champagne cocktail** Place a sugar lump in the glass and shake on a few drops of Angostura bitters, then add a dash of brandy and top up with champagne. **vodka martini** Swirl vermouth in a glass, then discard to next. Top with ice-shaken or frozen neat vodka and an olive.

the menu

teriyaki almonds vegan

Shimmering clusters of glazed, toasted nuts are utterly irresistible. These are the ideal bar snack: salty, sweet, and crunchy. You don't have to limit yourself to almonds—pecans, cashews, and Brazil nuts are all fantastic as well, though if you mix them, bear in mind that they may not cook evenly.

ingredients

scant 2 cups blanched whole almonds

3 tablespoons olive oil

2 tablespoons dark soy sauce

2 tablespoons mirin (Japanese cooking wine) or sweet sherry

$^1/_4$ teaspoon cayenne pepper

1 tablespoon sesame seeds

1 tablespoon superfine sugar

method

Preheat the oven to 400°F. Spread the almonds out on a baking tray and toast in the preheated oven for 5 minutes, until pale golden. Reduce the oven temperature to 300°F.

Combine the remaining ingredients in a bowl and mix well. Add the toasted almonds and stir to coat evenly. Pour the mixture back onto the baking tray and cook in the oven for about 20–25 minutes, stirring every 5 minutes. The liquid will reduce in the oven, eventually becoming a thick, dark, sticky coating that glazes the nuts.

Let the nuts cool on the baking tray. Use a metal spatula to scrape the nuts and glaze off the tray. Break up any large clumps, but leave some in little clusters. Arrange in a bowl and serve, with napkins nearby.

avocado & semidried tomato crostini vegan

The semidried tomato is the new sun-dried—it's softer, brighter, and juicier—but good old sun-dried tomatoes are fine, too. The spicy avocado purée is best made no more than four hours before serving.

ingredients

makes 20
olive oil, for brushing
20 (¹/2 in. thick) slices of very thin baguette
   or ciabatta
1 large or 2 small perfectly ripe avocados,
   pitted and peeled
juice of 1 lime
1 garlic clove, crushed

1 teaspoon ground cumin
¹/2 teaspoon hot chili powder, or to taste
salt and freshly ground black pepper
20 pieces semidried tomato in oil, drained
   (or use sun-dried)
fresh chives, cut into ³/4 in. lengths

method

To make the crostini, preheat the oven to 350°F. Brush a cookie sheet with olive oil, then place the bread slices on the sheet and drizzle lightly with olive oil. Bake in the preheated oven for about 10 minutes, until light golden and thoroughly crisp. Let cool, then keep in an airtight container until ready to use.

To make the avocado purée, mash the avocado with a potato masher until smooth, then mash in the lime juice, garlic, cumin, chili, salt, and pepper. Cover with plastic wrap and keep in the refrigerator until ready to use.

To assemble each canapé, place a small spoonful of avocado purée on each piece of bread. It looks best if not smoothed down too much. Place a semidried tomato on top and finish with a piece of chive.

artichoke toasties

People can never seem to get enough of these warm, crisp, and cheesy tartlets. They're ludicrously easy to make, so make more than you think you'll need. Using a high-quality loaf of bread for the bottom layer is a waste of money and effort—regular white sandwich bread is the key to their simplicity.

ingredients

makes 24

12 slices white sandwich bread

soft butter, for spreading

14 oz. can artichoke hearts, drained and chopped

2 oz. fresh Parmesan cheese, finely grated

2 fresh, fleshy, mild green chilies, seeded and finely chopped

3 heaping tablespoons mayonnaise

a pinch of salt

freshly ground black pepper

method

Preheat the oven to 425°F. Using a 2 in. wide glass tumbler or cookie cutter, cut two circles of bread out of each slice. Butter one side fairly generously and press butter-side down in a shallow nonstick muffin pan, flattening the entire surface with your fingertips.

Mix together the remaining ingredients, then place a spoonful of the mixture into each bread case, smoothing down the top evenly. Bake in the preheated oven for 12–15 minutes, until golden and crisp. Let cool briefly before slipping out of the pan. Serve warm.

eggplant & olive truffles

These look rather like little meatballs, though they practically float off the plate with lightness. Try to serve them as soon as possible out of the oven—like most hot snacks, their appeal is immediate. Once let loose on the guests, they won't have a hope of hanging around. The mixture can be made up to one day in advance.

ingredients

makes 24

1 large eggplant, approximately 1 lb. 2 oz.
2 tablespoons olive oil
1/2 cup pine nuts
20 Kalamata olives, pitted and chopped
4 tablespoons dry bread crumbs
6 tablespoons freshly grated Parmesan cheese, plus 2 tablespoons for sprinkling
2 tablespoons chopped fresh parsley
1 plump garlic clove, crushed
1 organic egg, beaten
butter, for greasing
to garnish (optional):
fresh parsley leaves
Parmesan cheese shavings

method

Preheat the oven to 450°F. Cut the eggplant in half lengthwise and brush with olive oil. Roast in the preheated oven for about 30 minutes, until golden and completely soft. Let cool, peel off the skin and discard, then chop the flesh finely. Reduce the oven temperature to 400°F.

Mix the eggplant flesh, pine nuts, olives, bread crumbs, Parmesan cheese, parsley, garlic, and egg together in a bowl, then let rest for 10–15 minutes.

Liberally grease a large cookie sheet. Form the mixture into bite-size balls and place on the sheet, then top each one with a pinch of grated Parmesan cheese.

Bake in the oven for 15–20 minutes, until golden and puffed up. Serve hot, with a few parsley leaves and Parmesan shavings sprinkled over the platter, if desired.

2

feed the masses

big bowls and platters that go a long way

Cooking for a crowd usually means it's celebration time—a wedding,

a big birthday, a graduation. For these occasions, sandwiches just won't do! Food is the life of the party, and if you're the cook, it can seem a little daunting, but it's also a lot of fun and immensely satisfying. Don't rely on a miracle; if you plan the menu sensibly and stay organized, everything will run as smooth as honey.

A stunning yet simple buffet is the best tactic for feeding crowds of people. Design a buffet with no more than four or five large dishes that can be eaten with a fork. They should have bold visual impact, presenting a contrast of textures, colors, and flavors. Choose one or two delicious nibbles to keep people happy before the buffet begins, but avoid anything that's complicated to make. Stick to one or two big desserts. Provide a backup of a giant cheese and bread tray. Bear in mind that hungry people are greedy at buffets and may take more than their fair share.

The irony of feeding the masses is that it takes almost the same amount of time to cook for 100 as it does for 1,000. Good food has to be fresh—so by nature it's ephemeral. The actual cooking can't be going on for much more than three days prior to the event. Solution? Delegation! Take on more pairs of hands than you think you need. Conserve energy and have the groceries delivered if you can. Assign one of the desserts to a friend or a local bakery, and buy prepackaged things such as petits fours and tart shells.

Finally, as the marathon begins, start with a well-rested body. Make a list of every task that needs to be done and check them off as you go. Take plenty of breaks—get some fresh air. Top tip: Drink water constantly, and don't forget to eat. You need to be firing on all cylinders!

Now, on your marks, get set...

tortellini skewers with herb oil

When cooking for large numbers, the smart entertainer will occasionally rely on a few items that are prepared by the pros (or by machine)—and this is a good example. Those hours of labor making homemade tortellini can be put to much better use. Delicious fresh pasta is widely available in major supermarkets, though if you can afford to be a little extravagant, get the tortellini made fresh at an Italian deli. These are perfect on a finger buffet; they're tempting, easy to eat, and quite substantial.

ingredients

makes 24 skewers

48 cheese-filled tortellini

10^1/$_2$ oz. mozzarella di bufala, *torn into coarse*
 chunks

24 high-quality pitted olives

12 sun-dried tomatoes in oil, each cut into two strips

for the oil:

approximately 20 fresh basil leaves

approximately 20 fresh Italian parsley leaves

^{1}/$_3$ cup extra-virgin olive oil

method

Wipe twenty-four bamboo skewers with a cloth to remove any splinters. Cook the tortellini in plenty of well-salted, boiling water until al dente. Drain, then rinse under delicately flowing cold water and spread out on a clean dish towel to dry.

Pair up a piece of cheese with an olive and wrap a strip of sun-dried tomato around them. Thread one tortellini onto a bamboo skewer, followed by the tomato-cheese-olive wrap, and finishing with a tortellini close to the end of the skewer. (If you're feeling lazy or rushed, thread them on as haphazardly as you like—they'll still taste scrumptious.) Keep the finished skewers covered in plastic wrap and chill in the refrigerator as soon as possible. Return to room temperature before serving.

To make the herb oil, blend the herbs and oil in a blender or spice grinder until fairly smooth. Arrange the skewers on a platter and drizzle with the herb oil just before serving.

think ahead

Assemble the skewers up to four hours in advance.

top tip

Buy more tortellini than you need, as some might fall apart in the cooking. Be careful not to overcook—they need to be really al dente. If you can't find buffalo milk mozzarella, use cow's, though not that rubbery pizza variety; settle for cubes of creamy Havarti or fontina instead.

serve with

These fit best into a buffet with a Mediterranean feel.

deluxe crudités

This sesame dip is the only dip I ever make. I am always asked to divulge the recipe, and people are amazed how something so simple could taste so divine. Even the person who loathes raw vegetables will manage to eat some with this stuff. The dip is best eaten on the day of preparation, as the sesame seeds tend to become soggy.

ingredients

serves 8–10

for the sesame dip:

¹/4 cup sesame seeds

generous ¹/2 cup strained plain or thick
* and creamy yogurt*

generous ¹/2 cup mayonnaise

3 tablespoons dark soy sauce

for the crudités (choose a selection of 4–5 items):

boiled baby new potatoes

blanched asparagus spears

Belgian endive leaves

trimmed radishes, a tiny bit of the top left intact

raw sugar snap peas

celery stalks from the heart, some leaves left on

baby carrots, trimmed

bite-size broccoli florets

bite-size cauliflower florets

sliced fennel

method

To make the dip, heat a dry skillet over moderate heat. Add the sesame seeds and toast, stirring until they are popping and lightly browned. Transfer to a bowl and let cool completely.

Combine the sesame seeds with the yogurt, mayonnaise, and soy sauce and mix very thoroughly. Transfer to a dipping bowl. Arrange the vegetables of your choice on a platter in individual clusters and serve with the sesame dip.

hot fennel salt vegan—A good complement to the creamy dip, this tastes particularly good with cherry tomatoes and cucumbers. It's potent stuff—a dab is all you need.

ingredients

1 tablespoon rock salt; 8 peppercorns; 1 teaspoon fennel seeds; 1 teaspoon coriander seeds; 1 small dried chili or ¹/2 teaspoon chili powder

method

Mix all the ingredients together in a spice grinder or use a mortar and pestle to work into a coarse powder. Transfer to a small, shallow bowl and serve.

green charbroiled antipasti platter

This blooming platter of succulent vegetables and marinated fresh mozzarella is magnetic—you can make a silly quantity and it's still guaranteed to vanish. You'll need one of those fabulous cast-iron ridged grill pans for this, ideally a large one that fits over two burners. A smoke-filled kitchen is inevitable (open the windows), but it's the smoke that works the magic on the vegetables. Alternatively, use an outdoor grill. Any vegetable responds well to this treatment, but root vegetables should be boiled first.

ingredients

serves 8–10

14 oz. green beans, trimmed

4 large or 8 small heads of Belgian endive,
*   halved lengthwise*

4 fennel bulbs, trimmed and cut into thick slices

2 heads of broccoli, stem peeled, cut into long pieces

4 tablespoons olive oil, plus a little extra-virgin
*   olive oil for drizzling*

salt and freshly ground black pepper

juice of 1–2 lemons

1 lb. 2 oz. mozzarella di bufala, *torn into thick shreds*

2 garlic cloves

1 teaspoon coarse sea salt

a handful of fresh Italian parsley, chopped

1 bunch of fresh basil, leaves torn

method

Heat a ridged grill pan over high heat for 10 minutes while you get started preparing the vegetables. Place one type of vegetable in a mixing bowl and drizzle lightly with olive oil, then use your hands to coat them all over. Cook one type of vegetable at a time until tender and nicely charred.

Once cooked, return each type of vegetable to the mixing bowl and season with salt and black pepper. Squeeze lemon juice over the beans, Belgian endive, and fennel while still hot. Avoid squeezing lemon juice over the broccoli as it may discolor. Let the vegetables cool, then store in plastic zip-seal bags in the refrigerator until required.

Place the torn mozzarella cheese in a large bowl. Pound the garlic with the salt in a mortar. Pound in the parsley until coarsely combined. Whisk in the olive oil and basil. Add the marinade to the mozzarella pieces and stir carefully, then chill in the refrigerator for at least 1 hour. Arrange the charred vegetables on a platter with the marinated mozzarella and serve immediately.

think ahead

This platter can be made up to one day in advance. Store the cooled vegetables in separate zip-seal plastic bags.

top tip

Buffalo mozzarella, made from buffalo's milk, is a luxury and is ideal for this recipe. If unavailable, use fresh cow's milk mozzarella, but not pizza mozzarella. Fresh mozzarella is very vulnerable to spoilage; keep it in the refrigerator until the last moment before combining with the marinade, then refrigerate until ready to serve.

serve with

Salad greens and plenty of fresh, crusty bread.

a celebration buffet

—A beautifully arranged buffet table will inspire lots of "oohs" and "aahs," which is so gratifying. Set it up so that it flows in one direction—left to right is the most logical. Start with a pile of plates at the top end, alongside cutlery wrapped in napkins. Don't squash the food platters up too much—give them room to breathe. Place the dish you anticipate being the most popular at the end of the buffet, which will discourage greed. Don't forget serving spoons, and use medium, not giant, ones.

For loose salad greens, instead of making a separate dressing, just drizzle some good-quality balsamic vinegar and olive oil directly on the greens and toss well with salt and black pepper.

shopping
If there's anything you can get delivered, go for it. Get all shopping out of the way the day before the celebration. If you're cooking over more than one day, try to buy everything in one shopping trip before you get started, but take any perishable items into consideration—look after fresh herbs and vegetables, and pack any dairy or other chilled items in the same bag. Use boxes to pack your food, making it easier to see what you have than when using a lot of bags.

presentation
If your budget can handle it, consider renting nice dishes and platters, then sending them back dirty for a small fee.

drinks
If you give people a choice between white wine and champagne, you can guess which one you'll run out of first! If you must limit your supply of bubbly, serve it alone first, then switch to wine. Get champagne flutes as well as wine goblets.

the menu

broccoli & lemon orzo vegan

Orzo is rice-shaped pasta with a toothsome bite. Here's a bright, citrus pasta salad that sings with fresh, green flavor. It's filling yet light, a meal in itself or a delicious accompaniment, making it an ideal buffet or potluck dish.

ingredients

serves 8–10

grated zest of 4 lemons

generous 3/4 cup fresh lemon juice
   (approximately 4 lemons)

4 shallots, finely sliced

salt and freshly ground black pepper

1 teaspoon superfine sugar

1/3 cup olive oil

1 large head of broccoli (approximately 1 lb. 2 oz.),
   cut into small florets, stem chopped

3 1/2 oz. snow peas, trimmed

1 lb. 2 oz. orzo

2 oz. pumpkin seeds

3 1/2 oz. raw sugar snap peas, sliced

a large handful of fresh Italian parsley, leaves stripped

20 semidried tomatoes in oil or 10 sun-dried tomatoes
   in oil, drained and cut into strips

method

Preheat the oven to 400°F. Bring a large pan of water to a boil and salt it well.

Place the lemon zest and juice in a bowl, add the shallots, salt, pepper, and sugar, then whisk in the olive oil. Set aside until required. (The shallots should soak in the dressing for a few minutes to become mild and soft.)

Blanch the broccoli and snow peas in the boiling water for 2 minutes. Remove with a perforated spoon or a strainer and plunge into a bowl of ice-cold water. Drain when the vegetables are cold.

Add the orzo to the pan and cook, stirring frequently, for 6–8 minutes or until al dente. Drain the orzo and rinse under cold running water until cool. Drain thoroughly and place in a large mixing bowl. Stir in the lemon shallot dressing. Set aside until required.

Place the pumpkin seeds on a cookie sheet and toast in the preheated oven for 5 minutes, until golden. Let cool.

Add the sugar snap peas, parsley, and semidried or sun-dried tomatoes to the bowl of orzo and mix thoroughly. Just before serving, stir in the broccoli, snow peas, and toasted pumpkin seeds.

think ahead

This dish can be made up to a day in advance, reserving the broccoli, snow peas, and pumpkin seeds to stir in just before serving.

sugarbeans vegan

Feeding the masses is made a lot easier by including these luscious legumes on the menu. They can be made ages in advance and only get better as the days go by. Like a really good chutney, they need time to mature, allowing the high quantity of sugar and vinegar to work their magic. They're also very cheap to make in quantity. Water chestnuts are the surprise ingredient in this salad, providing a welcome crunch against all those sweet, creamy beans.

ingredients

serves 10–12

for the salad:

1 lb. 2 oz. mixed dried beans

7 oz. green beans or string beans, cut into
   bite-size pieces

2 (8 oz.) cans water chestnuts, drained

1 green bell pepper, cut into bite-size pieces

1 red onion, sliced very finely

for the marinade:

1/2 cup balsamic vinegar

scant 1/2 cup superfine sugar

3 garlic cloves, crushed

2 teaspoons salt

freshly ground black pepper

1/2 cup olive oil

method

Soak the dried beans in plenty of cold water overnight, then drain and boil them in fresh water. Let them bubble furiously for 10 minutes, then simmer for 50 minutes, until tender but not falling apart too much. Alternatively, follow the package instructions. Do taste each type of bean to be sure they are all tender enough. Drain thoroughly.

Bring another small pan of water to a boil. Blanch the green beans for 2 minutes, drain, and rinse under cold running water or in a bowl of ice-cold water.

Meanwhile, prepare the marinade by whisking together all the ingredients except the olive oil. Beat in the olive oil gradually to emulsify.

Empty the drained cooked beans into a wide, shallow dish and pour the marinade over them while they are still hot. Let cool, then add the blanched green beans, water chestnuts, green bell pepper, and red onion. Stir thoroughly. Cover with plastic wrap and let chill in the refrigerator for at least 24 hours, preferably longer, stirring now and then. The salad will keep for several days in the refrigerator.

think ahead

This recipe should be made at least three days in advance and can be made up to four days in advance.

top tip

This recipe multiplies well, but portions decrease as the number of guests goes up. As part of a buffet containing several cold salads, I have fed 150 on eight times the recipe. For convenience, buy dried beans already packaged as mixed. The marinade can be made in a blender, but whisk in the oil by hand or else the dressing will appear unappetizingly cloudy.

seven-vegetable tagine vegan

Seven is for luck, and this tagine has never failed me. It's a riot of color and a symphony of flavor. Practically speaking, it's a caterer's dream. Roast the vegetables with whole spices until sweet and tender, then stir into a rich sauce. Walk away and leave it overnight to flourish . . . then all that's left to do is reheat and devour.

ingredients

serves 8–10

10½ oz. sweet potato, peeled and cut into chunks

10½ oz. carrots, peeled and cut into chunks

10½ oz. parsnips or celery root, peeled and
  cut into chunks

1 red and 1 yellow bell pepper, cut into chunks

1 large fennel bulb, cut into chunks

1 large red onion, cut into chunks

2 medium zucchini, cut into chunks

3 tablespoons olive oil

1 tablespoon cumin seeds

1 tablespoon fennel seeds

salt and freshly ground black pepper

for the sauce:

4 garlic cloves, chopped

3 tablespoons olive oil

14 oz. can chopped tomatoes

14 oz. can chickpeas, drained

1 cup full-bodied red wine

zest and juice of 1 orange

2 cinnamon sticks

12 pitted prunes, halved if large

to serve:

Parsley & Saffron Couscous (see below)

harissa (hot chili paste; optional)

thick yogurt (omit for vegans)

method

Preheat the oven to 425°F. Place all the vegetables in a roasting pan and coat with the olive oil, whole cumin and fennel seeds, salt, and pepper. Roast in the preheated oven for about 30 minutes, until soft and caramelized, stirring once or twice.

Meanwhile, to make the sauce, cook the garlic in olive oil. Add the remaining ingredients and simmer until thick. Remove from the heat and combine with the roasted vegetables. If you feel it is too thick, add a little water to achieve the desired consistency. Cover and let stand in a cool place overnight. Reheat until piping hot and serve with freshly cooked couscous, harissa, and yogurt.

parsley & saffron couscous vegan—Ideal with the tagine; great on its own.

ingredients

serves 8–10; ½ cup large golden raisins; 1 lb. 2 oz. couscous; 2 teaspoons saffron threads; 1 teaspoon salt; 1 cup whole almonds, toasted; 2 large handfuls of fresh Italian parsley leaves, left whole; grated zest and juice of 3 lemons; 6 tablespoons olive oil; freshly ground black pepper

method

Place the golden raisins in a bowl and soak in boiling water for 15–20 minutes, then drain and set aside. Combine the dry couscous, saffron, and salt in a large bowl and stir well. Pour in just enough boiling water to cover. Let swell for 5 minutes, then fluff thoroughly with a fork, separating each grain. Place the remaining ingredients in a large bowl and mix thoroughly with the soaked golden raisins and couscous. Season as necessary and serve immediately.

giant cheese & spinach pie

Here it is—the ultimate spanakopita recipe, which my friend Cathy Lowis has passed on from her Greek mother. This classic phyllo pie is an utterly perfect entertaining recipe—big, bold, and easy to multiply, it always succeeds in appealing to everyone and is usually the favorite dish of the meal. This version has a clever twist with a handful of rice.

ingredients

serve 10–12
for the filling:
2 tablespoons olive oil
6 scallions, white and green parts, chopped
1 lb. 10 oz. fresh spinach, washed and trimmed,
    or frozen leaf spinach
1 1/2 cups cottage cheese, drained of
    any excess whey
2 cups crumbled feta cheese

3 tablespoons chopped fresh dill
3 tablespoons chopped fresh parsley
1 tablespoon uncooked long-grain rice
salt and freshly ground black pepper
for the pie dough:
14 large sheets of phyllo pastry
6 tablespoons olive oil
1 1/2 sticks butter (6 oz.), melted

method

Preheat the oven to 350°F. To make the filling, heat the oil in a large pan over low to moderate heat. Add the scallions and cook until translucent and soft. Stir in the spinach and cook until just wilted. (If using frozen spinach, cook until heated through.) Drain in a colander and press out as much moisture as possible. Let cool, then place on a clean cloth, gather up the sides, and squeeze the excess moisture out of the spinach. Chop coarsely.

Combine the spinach with the remaining filling ingredients in a bowl and mix very thoroughly. Taste for seasoning— you may only need to add pepper, as the feta is salty enough.

Unwrap the phyllo pastry and, if necessary, cut to fit the bottom of a large, deep, rectangular baking pan or casserole dish. Cover the pastry with a barely damp cloth to prevent it from drying out and becoming brittle. Combine the olive oil and melted butter, then brush the butter mixture all over the baking pan or casserole dish. Place one layer of phyllo pastry on the bottom, brush with the melted butter mixture, top with another layer of phyllo pastry, brush with butter, and so on, forming seven layers. Spoon all of the filling on top, spreading it out evenly.

Continue layering the phyllo pastry on top of the filling, again forming seven layers. Brush the top with the melted butter mixture and then, using a very sharp knife, cut the phyllo pastry into serving-size diamond shapes (cut vertically down the center and then diagonally across) or squares.

Bake the pie in the preheated oven for 45 minutes to 1 hour, until sizzling, deep golden, and crisp right through each of the phyllo layers. Cut again along the original slits before serving.

think ahead

The filling can be made two days in advance. The whole cooked pie can be frozen, thawed, and reheated.

top tip

The filling has a tendency to be on the wet side, but by throwing in a handful of uncooked rice, any excess moisture is absorbed and the bottom stays quite crisp.

serve with

Salad and bread; Sugarbeans (page 38)

roasted asparagus & marbled egg platter

This is a particular favorite around Easter, when there is a lot to celebrate, including the start of the asparagus season! The extraordinary method of cooking eggs originates from an ancient Jewish recipe. Making the marbled eggs has become an absolute ritual for me every year, partly because of the fun of it, as well as the romance of the symbolism—fertility and rebirth. I usually slice and caramelize the leftover peeled onions and make soup or a savory tart.

ingredients

serves 12

12 yellow onions (not red or white)
12 organic eggs
3 tablespoons sunflower or corn oil
4–5 bunches of asparagus spears, trimmed
olive oil, for drizzling
salt and freshly ground black pepper

method

To make the marbled eggs, first peel the onions, reserving every bit of papery skin. Make a layer of onion skins in a pan and place the eggs on top, then cover with more onion skins, tucking them in between the eggs. Fill the pan with enough water to cover the eggs by at least $3/4$ in. depth. Add the sunflower oil and bring to a boil, then reduce to a simmer.

After about 30 minutes, lift the eggs out with a perforated spoon and whack gently with another spoon to crack the shells. Return to the onion dye bath and simmer very gently for 5–6 hours, topping up the water as necessary, though the oil will go some way toward preventing evaporation. Let the eggs cool in the liquid, then drain and peel to reveal a beautifully marbled surface. Keep in the refrigerator until ready to serve.

Preheat the oven to 425°F. To cook the asparagus, place the prepared spears in a roasting pan, drizzle over enough olive oil to just coat the surface, and use your hands to coat evenly. Roast the asparagus in the preheated oven for 10–15 minutes or until done to your taste—ideally until tender but maintaining a little bit of bite. Season to taste with salt and black pepper, then serve warm or cold with the marbled eggs.

think ahead

The eggs can be cooked up to two days in advance and the asparagus up to four hours in advance.

top tip

Snap off the bottom of the asparagus spears—they will break above the woody end, ensuring tenderness.

serve with

Sesame dip from the Deluxe Crudités, page 31

3

small courses
fantastic appetizers or components of a feast

The spiritual home of the small course is the entire sun-drenched, olive-rich region of

the Mediterranean. From tapas to meze, little dishes made of exquisite ingredients are designed to get the appetite stimulated on lazy evenings in the sunshine with a chilled glass of wine. Many of these traditional dishes are by default vegetarian—the fertility of the Mediterranean bears such a lush selection of ingredients. Prepared simply, the intention is to enhance the natural beauty of the key ingredient. Throughout the Mediterranean, they really know a thing or two when it comes to enjoying life through food.

In modern times, we aim to eat with a light and healthy approach as often as possible. We embrace the food of the Mediterranean for its healthy olive oil and vitamin-rich qualities as much as for its sunny flavors. We can also embrace the custom of exciting the appetite and keeping it aroused with every small course, rather than extinguishing it with a big, heavy one. This is a rich tradition in Asia as well; at street markets you can enjoy "little eats"—hopping from stall to stall, trying a little bit at each one. It's a far more interesting way to eat, and when you are entertaining, it's an exciting way to cook.

All the recipes in this chapter can be enjoyed as the opening of a fantastic meal, as the components of a feast of little dishes, or simply on their own as a light meal. They can all be served from one platter or bowl, or as individual treats. If you are feeding many, you might wish to prepare individual dishes and have them waiting on the table before the meal begins. Every host should want to spoil the guests, but be judicious with multiple courses and space them out sensibly—that way every bite will be appreciated.

spiced baby eggplants with minted yogurt

Indian cooks are fond of stuffing baby eggplants, and these are cooked in the style of southern India, filling the house with a rich curry fragrance. Choose teardrop-shaped eggplants, about 2½ in. long, and cook them up to six hours in advance, combining with the sauce just before serving.

ingredients

serves 4–6

1 lb. 2 oz. baby eggplants

1¼ cups vegetable stock

for the spice oil:

5 tablespoons sunflower or corn oil

2 teaspoons black mustard seeds

4 garlic cloves, finely chopped

2–3 fresh red chilies, finely chopped

1 teaspoon ground turmeric

2 teaspoons cumin seeds

½ teaspoon fenugreek seeds (optional)

½ teaspoon salt

for the sauce:

generous ⅓ cup thick yogurt

a handful of fresh mint, chopped

juice of 1 lime

salt and freshly ground black pepper

method

First make the spice oil. Heat the oil in a nonstick skillet over moderate to high heat. Add the mustard seeds and when they start to pop, stir in the remaining ingredients. Immediately take the skillet off the heat and pour the oil into a cold ceramic bowl. Let the oil cool. Wipe the cooled skillet with paper towels, leaving a light slick of oil.

Meanwhile, prepare the eggplants. Grip by the stem end and lay on a cutting board, then, using a very sharp knife, slice the flesh from top to bottom, leaving the stem intact, making three or four thin slices. Alternatively, cut them into fourths, again leaving the stem intact.

When the spice oil is cool, use a teaspoon to apply a little oil and spice in between each layer of the sliced eggplants. Secure each one at the bottom with a toothpick or wooden skewer. Arrange them in the reheated skillet and cook over moderate heat until lightly colored on one side, then turn over and color the other side. Pour in the vegetable stock, cover, and reduce the heat to a simmer. Cook for about 10–15 minutes, until very soft—when prodded with a skewer they should offer no resistance. Remove the lid and increase the heat slightly, and reduce any remaining juices to a thick glaze that just coats the bottom of the pan.

To make the sauce, combine all the ingredients, then spread the sauce on a plate, place the eggplants on top, and drizzle any pan juices over them. Serve warm or cold.

raw thai salad in a pappadam shell vegan

This salad is all crunch and perfume—it really gets the appetite stirring, while being exceptionally light. I created it for a friend's summer wedding. The colorful salads were waiting at each place setting, forming part of the decoration as the guests came into the lavishly floral wedding tent. It's simple enough to produce in large quantities easily, but also works well for a smaller, less formal affair.

ingredients

serves 8–10

for the dressing:

1/3 cup corn syrup

2 tablespoons lime juice

1/4 cup light soy sauce

2 garlic cloves

2–3 small, fresh red chilies, sliced

3 lemongrass sticks, sliced (optional)

4 kaffir lime leaves, stem removed and coarsely chopped (optional)

for the salad:

scant 2 cups shredded red cabbage

1 red bell pepper, seeded and sliced

2 cups bean sprouts

8 scallions, sliced diagonally

2 (7 oz.) cans sliced water chestnuts, drained

4 canned hearts of palm, drained and sliced diagonally

4 fresh mint sprigs, leaves stripped

oil, for deep-frying

10 pappadams

10 leaves from a round lettuce, washed and thoroughly dried

3 tablespoons sesame seeds, toasted

2 limes, cut into wedges

8–10 edible flowers, such as pansies or nasturtiums (optional)

method

To make the dressing, mix everything in the blender until smooth and set aside until required. Toss the first seven salad ingredients together lightly and keep cool.

Fill a deep skillet with 4 in. of oil and heat until it starts to smoke (375°F). Using tongs, carefully place a pappadam in the oil, then use a ladle to press down in the center—the pappadam will form a basket around the ladle. Drain upside down on paper towels. Repeat with the other pappadams and allow to cool.

Line each cooled pappadam with a lettuce leaf. Toss the dressing through the vegetables and spoon into each basket. Sprinkle with the toasted sesame seeds and finish with a lime wedge and an edible flower (if using).

think ahead

Pappadam shells can be fried four hours in advance and kept in a dry place.

ginger-spiked avocados vegan

If there is a way to improve the heavenly, buttery flavor of ripe avocados, then this is it. Ginger and avocado have a surprising affinity. Prepare these as close to serving time as you can.

ingredients

serves 6
3 perfectly ripe avocados
juice of 1–2 lemons
2 tablespoons dark soy sauce
1 tablespoon balsamic vinegar
2 teaspoons finely grated fresh root ginger
freshly ground black pepper
sprigs of dill, to garnish

method

Slice the avocados in half and remove the pits. To extract a complete half from the skin, soak a large spoon in a cup of boiling water for a few seconds, then use it to quickly slide between the skin and the flesh at the narrow end of the avocado. The warmth of the spoon should "melt" the flesh slightly, allowing you to scoop the avocado flesh out in one smooth move. Alternatively, cut the avocados into fourths and peel away the skin. Sprinkle lemon juice over the avocados and use your hands to gently coat them all over. Place on a platter or individual serving plates.

Mix together the soy sauce, vinegar, and ginger and drizzle over the avocados or pour into the pit cavity. Finish with a good grinding of black pepper and decorate with sprigs of dill.

roasted spiced squash soup with tamarind vegan

Imagine if velvet could bite, and you get some idea of what this soup tastes like. Buy a dense-fleshed squash weighing about 3 lb. for the recipe, to allow for peeling and seeding.

ingredients

serves 4–6

2 lb. squash flesh, peeled and cut into chunks

1 teaspoon coriander seeds

1 teaspoon cumin seeds

6 garlic cloves

2¹/₂ in. piece of fresh root ginger, peeled and chopped

salt and freshly ground black pepper

3–4 tablespoons extra-virgin olive oil

4 cups vegetable stock

2 tablespoons tamarind cream (page 17) or

   1 tablespoon brown sauce or 2 teaspoons

   Worcestershire sauce

to garnish (optional):

heavy cream or plain yogurt

hulled squash seeds

method

Preheat the oven to 400°F. Place the squash in a roasting pan and sprinkle with the spices, whole garlic cloves, ginger, salt, and black pepper. Drizzle the olive oil on top and toss with your hands to coat evenly. Roast in the preheated oven for 30–40 minutes, stirring once or twice, until the squash is very soft.

Let cool slightly, then scrape into a pan and add the vegetable stock and tamarind cream. Bring to a boil and simmer very gently for 10 minutes. Process into a totally smooth purée, then serve in warm bowls with a drizzle of cream or yogurt and squash seeds sprinkled over the top.

beet & coconut soup vegan

This soup is an absolute stunner. Coconut and beets are often cooked together in southern India, which is the inspiration for this exciting soup. The shocking pink beets are made even brighter on a canvas of milky coconut—and the exotic flavors really do match up to the brilliant appearance. Any soup can be served as a canapé out of tiny espresso cups or shot glasses (allow the soup to cool slightly before pouring into delicate cups or glasses). This one is particularly impressive served in this way.

ingredients

serves 4–6

1 lb. 2 oz. fresh beets, leaves removed, scrubbed

7 oz. block of creamed coconut, chopped

4 cups vegetable stock

4 garlic cloves, peeled, coarsely chopped or halved

1 teaspoon ground cumin

grated zest of 1 lemon

juice of 1/2 lemon

to serve:

Cucumber Salsa (see below)

pita breads or chapatis, cut into strips and toasted

method

Bring a large pan of water to a boil and salt it well. Add the beets and boil for 30–40 minutes, until tender throughout (test with a skewer or sharp knife). Drain, then rinse under cold running water and rub off the skins, tops, and spindly roots. Chop coarsely.

Bring the vegetable stock to a boil in the rinsed-out pan, then stir in the coconut until dissolved.

Place the chopped beets, garlic, cumin, lemon zest and juice, and 3/4 cup water in a blender and process until smooth.

Add the beet purée to the boiling coconut stock. (You can swirl some coconut stock around the blender to get out every last bit of purée.) Bring to a boil and simmer for 10 minutes. Serve in warm bowls with a spoonful of Cucumber Salsa on top, with strips of toasted pita bread or chapati on the side.

cucumber salsa vegan—a clean-tasting salsa that lightens up the soup.

ingredients

2 in. piece of cucumber, peeled, seeded, and very finely chopped; 1 shallot, finely chopped; 10 fresh mint leaves, finely chopped; 1 fresh red chili, seeded and finely chopped; a squeeze of lemon juice; a pinch of salt

method

Simply mix all the ingredients together thoroughly. It benefits from standing for awhile, allowing the flavor to develop.

a small feast for friends

—For a laid-back weekend afternoon with friends, escape from the routine appetizer-main-dessert format—try a casual six-course meal. If you think that sounds like a contradiction in terms, think again. It's an invitation to eat lavishly, but informally. I promise you won't be shopping, chopping, and washing up for days.

The idea is simple: Six consecutive small dishes, each to be considered and savored, one after the other. Choose six simple recipes, including something sweet. Some courses could be as simple as boiled artichokes with lemon and mayonnaise, a bowl of twinkling olives, or slices of sensuous, ripe mango. Don't reveal the menu. It's fun to maintain a sense of excitement and curiosity between courses.

shopping   Seek out an unusual food store or deli in the morning or the day before. Don't be rigid about your menu. Go with an open mind—you might find a special cheese, some irresistible tomatoes as sweet as cherries, or a bizarre morsel you've never discovered before for everyone to sample.

presentation   You won't need six sets of dishes for this six-course affair. One or two small plates and maybe one small bowl per person will suffice. Don't even think about washing dishes until after everyone leaves—or the next day.

drinks   Beer seems to encourage laughter more than other drinks. Try buying a selection of different types of beer and ale and sampling a new one with each course. If it's a hot day, serve the beer in chilled glass mugs.

the menu

avocado soup with toasted cheese topping

The avocado is a sensuous and moody creature. When overripe, its incredible buttery texture can almost forgive a slightly off flavor. When underripe, it's totally inedible. Avocados are vulnerable—rough handling destroys them, as does fierce heat. However, as they have the highest fat content of all fruits, a careful warming brings out the best in them. This recipe, inspired by a soup I ate in Mexico, is essentially a guacamole diluted with hot stock. It's a breeze to make, but be careful not to cook it—merely warm it through.

ingredients

serves 4–6

for the soup:

4 medium ripe avocados

juice of 2 limes

generous 3/4 cup crème fraîche or sour cream

1 small onion, finely chopped

2 tomatoes, chopped

1 garlic clove, crushed

1 fresh red chili, seeded and finely chopped

salt and freshly ground black pepper

3 cups hot vegetable stock

for the topping:

3 1/2 oz. corn tortilla chips (unflavored)

1 cup grated cheddar or Monterey Jack cheese

4 scallions, chopped

1/2 cup crème fraîche or sour cream

method

Preheat the oven or broiler to its highest setting. Scoop out the avocado flesh and mash it with the lime juice. (A potato masher is the perfect tool for the job.) Stir in the crème fraîche or sour cream, onion, tomato, garlic, and chili and season to taste with salt and black pepper. Place the individual serving bowls on an oven tray and slide them into the oven to warm slightly.

The stock should be hot but not boiling. Stir the stock into the avocado mixture, then ladle into the warmed serving bowls. To make the topping, sprinkle a few tortilla chips on top of each bowl and sprinkle with the grated cheese. Put the bowls in the oven or under the broiler for just a few minutes, until the cheese melts. To serve, top with a few chopped scallions and a dollop of crème fraîche or sour cream and eat immediately.

think ahead

The avocado mixture can be made up to two hours in advance. Cover with plastic wrap and keep in the refrigerator, then bring up to room temperature before adding to the stock.

top tip

Presentation is most impressive out of individual bowls, but you can also pour the soup into one large ovenproof dish, allowing plenty of surface area for sprinkling the tortillas and cheese, then serve from the dish.

serve with

This is quite a filling soup and can be made into a complete meal with a salad on the side.

warm mushroom salad with creamy caper dressing

Use any mushroom you fancy for this simple yet sophisticated salad. It's easily converted to a main course by adding hard-boiled eggs or fried haloumi cheese.

ingredients

serves 4

2 tablespoons butter

1 tablespoon olive oil

2 garlic cloves, sliced

14 oz. exotic mushrooms or cremini or portobello
   mushrooms, stems removed, thinly sliced

salt and freshly ground black pepper

3 tablespoons finely chopped mixed herbs, such as
   rosemary, sage, thyme, marjoram, and parsley

grated zest and juice of 1 lemon

7 oz. mixed lettuce leaves

crusty bread, to serve

for the dressing:

1/2 cup crème fraîche or sour cream

2 tablespoons capers in vinegar, plus 1 teaspoon
   caper vinegar

1 tablespoon snipped fresh chives

1–2 tablespoons water, optional

method

Melt the butter in a large skillet or preheated wok over moderate heat and add the olive oil. Add the garlic and cook until fragrant. Add the mushrooms and season well with salt and black pepper. Stir-fry until the mushrooms are soft, then add the herbs and cook for about 5 minutes, until most of the pan juices have evaporated. Squeeze the juice of half a lemon over the mushroom mixture and remove from the heat.

To make the dressing, combine all the ingredients with the remaining lemon juice and zest. If desired, thin slightly with the water. Spoon the warm mushroom mixture over the mixed lettuce leaves and drizzle with the dressing. Serve with bread.

honey-roast parsnip & pear salad with blue cheese dressing

Parsnips, pears, and any blue cheese are a harmonious trio. This is an elegant winter salad that starts off a meal in style. It's well-balanced nutritionally, with the buttery macadamia nuts for extra protein, so it can also be served as a light main course.

ingredients

serves 4

4 small parsnips, peeled and cut into fourths lengthwise

2 tablespoons olive oil

1 tablespoon honey

salt and freshly ground black pepper

4 handfuls of arugula

2 dessert pears (such as Bartlett), sliced into wedges

3/4 cup macadamia nuts, toasted

for the dressing:

5 1/2 oz. Gorgonzola or other strong blue cheese

3 tablespoons white wine vinegar

1/2 cup olive oil

method

Preheat the oven to 400°F. Place the parsnips in a roasting pan and coat with the olive oil. Drizzle with the honey and season to taste with salt and black pepper. Roast in the preheated oven for about 20 minutes, until golden. Let cool.

To make the dressing, mash the Gorgonzola in a bowl. Stir in the vinegar and whisk in the olive oil with a little salt and black pepper until fairly smooth.

Arrange the arugula on individual plates and follow with the pears, toasted nuts, and roasted parsnips, then pour the dressing on top. Finish with more black pepper.

no-knead honey seed bread

If you love bread with a granular texture, you'll love it even more having made it yourself. To make this sturdy loaf, you will have to get your hands stuck in, but very little elbow grease is required. Seek out hemp seeds—available from health-food stores—they have a wonderful, nutty crunch, a bit like popcorn.

ingredients

serves 6–8

2 tablespoons honey

1 tablespoon active dry yeast

2 cups whole-wheat flour

1 1/2 cups all-purpose flour

2 teaspoons salt

2 tablespoons hulled pumpkin seeds

2 tablespoons hulled sunflower seeds

2 tablespoons hemp seeds

butter, for greasing

milk, for brushing (optional)

1 tablespoon poppy seeds, for sprinkling (optional)

method

Dissolve the honey in 1 1/4 cups hot (but not boiling) water in a small bowl or pitcher. Whisk in the yeast and let stand in a warm place for about 15 minutes, until frothy.

Combine the two flours in a mixing bowl. Using a wooden spoon, stir in the salt and the pumpkin, sunflower, and hemp seeds. Gradually add the yeasty water and mix to a dough. As the dough draws together, put the spoon aside and start using one hand to press the dough into a ball and the other hand to turn the bowl, incorporating everything into a soft, pliable mixture that leaves the sides of the bowl fairly clean. If the mixture is very sticky, sprinkle in a bit of flour to form a soft dough; if it is dry, sprinkle in a few drops of water and work it through until the flour disappears.

Grease a cookie sheet. Place the dough on it and form into a tapered "eye" shape—or whatever shape you fancy. Dust with flour and cover with a damp dish towel. Let rise in a warm place for about 1 hour, until doubled in size. Preheat the oven to 400°F. Use kitchen scissors to make decorative snips down the middle of the bread. Brush all over with milk and sprinkle with poppy seeds, if desired. Bake the loaf in the preheated oven for 30–40 minutes, until golden, firm, and hollow-sounding when tapped. Let cool on a wire rack.

hot brie fondue—If you're fortunate enough to have access to a serious cheese shop, ask for the *Vacherin du Mont d'Or Sancey Richard*, which is perfect for this treatment. The same method will work with any soft, mature cheese with a washed rind, ideally in a box. If there's no box, you can still wrap the cheese itself in foil—the objective is a hot package of sinfully creamy goo to dip the bread in.

ingredients

serves 6–8; *mature soft cheese in a box; a little white wine*

method

Preheat the oven to 400°F. Take the lid off the cheese and drizzle a little white wine over the rind. Replace the lid and wrap the cheese in its box in foil. Place in the preheated oven on the middle rack for 15–20 minutes, after which time the cheese should be liquified right through. Unwrap and dunk slices of the Honey Seed Bread into the warm, runny cheese.

4

lunch & dinner meals

main dishes, some to serve with all the trimmings

The vegetarian main course seems to be the biggest stumbling block of all for the inexperienced. If you've planned a meal that revolves around a joint of meat, what do you do for the vegetarian? How do you create a meat substitute?

The answer is—don't. Soy-based "mock meat" products just don't fit the bill, and the days of the nut roast are now firmly behind us. Most vegetarians will be happy with all the trimmings of a roast, like potatoes and vegetables, supplemented with a dish that has lots of flavor and, ideally, a little protein. All of the dishes in this chapter can be slotted into that format. Don't forget, however, that many people will want to share the veggie dish! Make enough to go around the table—it's no fun to be alienated as the lone vegetarian.

A more interesting way of designing a menu is to give all the elements of the meal equal focus. If meat is being served, let it be one of the elements, but not the main event. Choose four or five dishes that balance each other perfectly. Provide a range of textures, for instance something crisp or crunchy, like lightly cooked green beans with toasted almonds, to contrast with a soft and creamy food like mashed potatoes. Avoid serving foods that are all the same color, especially brown. Consider the various tastes and aim to balance sweet and sour elements. Always serve one very clean-tasting dish, such as a simple salad or a steamed green vegetable, especially if the rest of the meal is very salty or spicy.

Avoid overcomplicating matters, however, especially if you're only cooking for a few. All the dishes in this chapter can, of course, be served as meals on their own.

ricotta & herb dumplings with vodka & cèpe butter sauce

The Italians would call these dumplings *malfatti*, meaning "badly made," because they are irregular in an endearing kind of way, meaning less fuss for the cook. The vodka fleshes out the sauce and turns this into a seriously good dish. It could easily be slotted into a roast meal—serve from a sizzling casserole on a wooden board, or transfer to a warm serving dish to be passed around with freshly grated Parmesan.

ingredients

serves 4

10½ oz. baby spinach, washed

2–6 tablespoons all-purpose flour

a large handful of fresh herbs, such as basil, parsley,
*   or oregano, chopped*

1 lb. 2 oz. ricotta cheese, drained

3 eggs

2 oz. fresh Parmesan cheese, grated

2 tablespoons semolina

salt and freshly ground black pepper

for the sauce:

1 tablespoon dried cèpes (approximately ¼ oz.)

¾ stick butter (3 oz.)

2 garlic cloves, chopped

⅓ cup vodka

freshly grated Parmesan cheese, to serve

method

First prepare the cèpes for the sauce. Place them in a bowl and pour in enough boiling water to cover. Let soak for 15 minutes, then drain, rinse again, and chop. For the dumplings, bring a large pan of salted water to a boil, then reduce to a simmer.

Meanwhile, place the spinach in a colander and pour boiling water directly over until it is wilted, then drain well, pressing out as much moisture as you can. Squeeze in a clean cloth to dry out further. Place the spinach in a food processor with the remaining ingredients—start with 2 tablespoons flour and pulse until well mixed. Alternatively, chop the spinach and herbs, then beat with the other ingredients in a bowl. The mixture should have the consistency of cottage cheese—it should just drop off the spoon.

The water in the pan should be simmering gently. Drop one test spoonful of the mixture into the water—don't panic if it falls apart, just add more flour to the mixture, then drop in spoonfuls and boil until they rise to the top, about 2–3 minutes. Drain thoroughly in a colander lined with paper towels. Cook in batches and keep warm in a dish in the oven.

To make the sauce, melt the butter in a skillet. Add the garlic and prepared cèpes and cook for 2 minutes. Add the vodka and season to taste with salt and pepper. Return to a boil, then simmer for 2 minutes, until the alcohol fumes are gone. Spoon over the dumplings and be generous with the Parmesan.

broiled tofu & mango skewers vegan

Anyone who doesn't like tofu should consider this: It just needs a little TLC to transform it from boring to irresistible. Cooking in hot oil gives it a crisp texture, and marinating kicks its spongy talents into action as it drinks up a pungent sauce.

ingredients

serves 4–5

for the sauce:

4 tablespoons dark soy sauce
2 tablespoons corn syrup or honey
1 tablespoon chili sauce or 5–6 dashes Tabasco sauce
2 tablespoons lime juice
1 tablespoon finely grated fresh root ginger

for the skewers:

4 tablespoons cornstarch
10½ oz. tofu, drained and patted dry
vegetable oil, for pan-frying
1 small, ripe but firm mango, cubed
10 kaffir lime leaves (optional)
10 lime wedges

method

Pour boiling water over ten long wooden skewers and let cool; this should prevent them from burning on the broiler. Mix together the sauce ingredients and set aside.

Sprinkle the cornstarch over a plate. Cut the tofu into twenty ½ in. chunks and roll in the cornstarch, shaking off any excess. Heat about a ½ in. depth of oil in a wide skillet until hot but not smoking. Cook the tofu, turning once with tongs, until crisp and golden all over. Keep the pieces from touching or they may stick together. Drain on paper towels briefly, then transfer to a plate. Spoon half the sauce over the hot tofu and let cool. If you have time, it will improve further if marinated for 1–2 hours in the refrigerator.

Thread a piece of mango, a piece of tofu, a lime leaf (if using), another piece of tofu, mango, and finishing with a lime wedge onto each skewer. Heat a ridged grill pan over high heat or heat the oven broiler to high. Broil the skewers, using tongs to turn them, until lightly charred all over. If the pan is hot, the cooking process should be quick, as the tofu is already fried. Use any remaining sauce to flavor accompanying noodles or rice.

smoked eggplant relish vegan—A sensational complement to the skewers.

ingredients

1 long, thin eggplant; ¼ cucumber, seeded and diced; a handful of fresh chives, snipped; 1 fresh green chili, seeded and chopped; 2 tablespoons chopped fresh mint; 1 tablespoon fresh lime juice; 1 tablespoon light soy sauce; 1 teaspoon superfine sugar

method

Push a fork into the stem of the eggplant and carefully place the body directly onto a high gas flame. Turn the eggplant occasionally until completely soft and collapsed; the skin should be blackened to the point of ash in places, and steam should be escaping through the fork holes. Alternatively, prick with a fork and broil until blistered all over.

Transfer to a plate and let cool, then peel off the charred skin and chop up the flesh. Don't worry if a few little charred bits remain, as they will add to the flavor. Combine the flesh with the remaining ingredients and serve.

sweet potato gnocchi with dolcelatte sauce

Gnocchi, the classic Italian potato dumplings, can be a little stodgy, so here's a new twist. Orange-fleshed sweet potato lightens them up beautifully. This minimalist cheese sauce is rather sinful, but goes outrageously well with sweet potato. When choosing sweet potato, rub a tiny speck of the skin off to be sure the flesh is orange. This is a rich dish and a little goes a long way—small portions are best; it's also very appetizing as a first course.

ingredients

serves 4–6

for the gnocchi:

1 lb. 2 oz. orange-fleshed sweet potato, scrubbed
salt and freshly ground black pepper
2 egg yolks
heaping 1/2 cup all-purpose flour
1/3 cup semolina, plus extra for dusting

for the sauce:

2/3 cup light cream
7 oz. dolcelatte or Gorgonzola cheese, cubed

method

Preheat the oven to 425°F. Prick the sweet potatoes and roast in the preheated oven for 45 minutes to 1 hour, until soft. Let stand until cool enough to handle, then peel.

Mash the flesh with a potato masher and fold in the remaining ingredients. Using wet hands, roll the dough into little dumplings and place on a large cookie sheet dusted with semolina. Bring a large pan of salted water to a boil, drop the dumplings into the boiling water, and boil until they rise to the surface, about 3–4 minutes, then drain.

To make the sauce, heat the cream gently to boiling and stir in the cheese until it melts. Grind in some black pepper and serve immediately, poured over the gnocchi.

roasted eggplants & haloumi with almond sauce

Based on a fifteenth-century Italian recipe, this exotic-tasting sauce uses pomegranate molasses, an amazing sweet-and-sour syrup made from pure concentrated juice. It is also delicious drizzled over soft white salty cheese.

ingredients

serves 4

2 medium eggplants

olive oil, for brushing

salt and freshly ground black pepper

9 oz. haloumi cheese, thinly sliced
   (vegans: use tempeh)

10¹/₂ oz. baby spinach, washed

a handful of fresh mint leaves, torn

for the sauce:

4 tablespoons ground almonds

1 tablespoon pomegranate molasses
   (or 1 tablespoon balsamic vinegar) blended with
   4 tablespoons water

1 teaspoon superfine sugar

1 teaspoon cinnamon

1 teaspoon grated fresh root ginger

1 small garlic clove, crushed

method

Preheat the oven to 425°F. Cut the stem end off the eggplants and discard, then cut into four long wedges. Score the flesh in one diagonal direction, without piercing the skin. Brush thoroughly with olive oil and season to taste with salt and black pepper. Roast for 15–20 minutes, until soft and golden. Keep warm.

Now cook the cheese in a dry skillet until golden on both sides. To make the sauce, pound everything together in a mortar until smooth. If allowed to stand, the sauce will thicken; dilute with more water if necessary—it should have the consistency of creamy hummus. Arrange the spinach on a serving plate, then top with the cooked eggplant and cheese. Spoon the sauce on top or on the side. Sprinkle the torn mint on top and serve.

truffle-scented stuffed mushrooms

Wild about mushrooms? Well, here's a real fungi-fest. There's something so seductive about the deep, dark hue, rich flavor, and a texture that can only be described as, well, meaty.

ingredients

serves 6, or 3 generous servings of two mushrooms each

6 medium portobello, flat, or cremini mushrooms, similar in size, plus an extra 5 1/2 oz.

2 tablespoons olive oil, plus extra for brushing

2 tablespoons truffle oil, plus an extra 1 1/2 tablespoons

salt and freshly ground black pepper

9 oz. shiitake mushrooms, stems removed

5 garlic cloves, sliced

1/2 cup Madeira wine, sherry, or vermouth

2 teaspoons fresh thyme leaves

a good grinding of nutmeg

2 oz. fresh Parmesan cheese, grated

a generous handful of fresh Italian parsley leaves

method

Preheat the oven to 400°F. Cut the stems out of the six stuffing mushrooms, then brush the caps generously with olive oil and lay gill-side up on a cookie sheet. Drizzle a teaspoon truffle oil over the gills of each mushroom and season to taste with salt and black pepper. Coarsely chop the remaining mushrooms, including the shiitakes.

Heat the olive oil in a skillet. Add the garlic and cook for a couple of minutes until fragrant. Add the chopped portobello and shiitake mushrooms, salt, and a generous grinding of black pepper. Cook over medium-high heat until the mushrooms have collapsed. Pour in the Madeira wine, add the thyme and nutmeg, increase the heat, and cook until the juices have mostly evaporated. Let cool briefly, then place in a food processor with the grated Parmesan, parsley, and the remaining truffle oil. Process until a purée results, then spoon the mixture into the mushroom hollows and bake in the preheated oven for 20–30 minutes, until shrunken and lightly golden on top.

think ahead   The filling can be made twenty-four hours in advance.

top tip   If you are fortunate enough to have a fresh truffle, by all means use it—1 tablespoon of shavings in the filling
mixture would be enough, plus a little more shaved over the finished article. In lieu of truffle oil you could also use
1–2 tablespoons of truffle paste, sold as "salsa truffina." I don't recommend truffles in brine.

serve with   Delicious with cornbread, especially broiled, for added bite; or bruschetta, to accommodate the juices. These go
beautifully with the trimmings for a roast meal.

a fancy Sunday roast

The Sunday roast is a bit of a dinosaur, but it's not yet extinct. It's a valuable ritual of family security, when loved ones gather to share gossip, relive old tales, and revel in unlimited comfort food. All too often these days, it's reserved for holidays like Thanksgiving and Christmas, but it could be welcomed any weekend. These occasions should be spoiling, but never strenuous; dinner's ready when it's ready. Relax and have fun introducing a little adventure into the traditional menu.

Roast potatoes are an absolute must-have for this menu, and here's the winning formula: Peel potatoes and boil for 5–10 minutes, until slightly floury on the outside but hard in the middle, then drain. Shake them around in a roasting pan to rough them up, coat with plenty of olive oil, season, and roast in a 425°F oven for 40–50 minutes until golden brown and crispy.

shopping   This is an indisputably wintry menu, characterized by the seasonal, rib-clinging ingredients and substantial cooking time. Shopping might involve a trip to an outdoor market. If you've got several guests coming, make your life easier and delegate shopping or even whole cooked dishes.

presentation If you've got a fine set of china, now's the time to get it out. Polish the silver, shine the glasses, light the candles, and relish the ritual.

drinks   A top-notch, full-bodied red wine is the ideal choice. A moderately priced Shiraz or Rioja seems to go miles further than inferior wine, as every sip is savored.

the menu

gratin of roasted garlic & squash *80*

ricotta & herb dumplings with vodka & cèpe butter sauce *67*

roast potatoes *74*

steamed tender-stem broccoli

radicchio & tomato salad drizzled with balsamic vinegar

cranberry torte with hot toffee-brandy sauce *90*

simple asparagus tarts

I affectionately call these "asparagus in a frame." I first devised this recipe for a large party on a minuscule budget, to be inexpensive (it was asparagus season) as well as easy to prepare. Afterward, I got calls from many of the guests, asking me to make them one or two, which I gladly agreed to because they only take ten minutes to make.

ingredients

serves 4–8

1 lb. 2 oz. medium-thickness asparagus spears, trimmed

2 teaspoons semolina or cornmeal

13 oz. ready-rolled puff pastry

2 egg yolks

scant 1/2 cup crème fraîche or sour cream

a pinch of salt

freshly ground black pepper

heaping 1/2 cup freshly grated Parmesan cheese

method

Preheat the oven to 425°F. Bring a pan of salted water to a boil. Add the asparagus, return to a boil, and cook for 3 minutes. Drain under cold running water until cool, then pat dry.

Sprinkle the semolina or cornmeal over a large cookie sheet, or over two small ones. Divide the puff pastry into two rectangles and place on the sheet. Using a sharp knife, score a 3/4 in. border around the edge of the pastry, not cutting through completely. Arrange the asparagus inside the pastry frames. To ensure that each slice has a fair share of the delicious tips, alternate the direction of the tips. Mix together the egg yolks, crème fraîche or sour cream, and seasoning in a measuring glass. Pour the mixture evenly into the middle of the two pastry frames, which should allow the borders to puff up in the oven before the custard runs off the edge. Quickly sprinkle the Parmesan over the two pastries and place in the preheated oven immediately.

Bake for 20–30 minutes, until the pastry is deep golden and the custard is patched with gold. Serve warm, each tart cut into four pieces. Cold tarts can be successfully reheated in an oven at 400°F for 5–7 minutes.

potato, garlic, & smoked mozzarella strudel

Strudel literally means "whirlwind," but this one is a breeze to make. Ready-made puff pastry is an honorable convenience, and when ready-rolled is easy to use. All-butter pastry has the best flavor and flakiest texture.

ingredients

serves 6–8

1 lb. 10 oz. mealy potatoes (such as Russet),
    peeled and cut into chunks

3 small garlic cloves

1 teaspoon coarse sea salt

9 oz. smoked mozzarella, or other smoked cheese,
    cut into 1/2 in. cubes

3–4 tablespoons finely chopped, fresh Italian parsley

freshly ground black pepper

13 oz. ready-rolled puff pastry

1 egg yolk mixed with 1 tablespoon milk, for glazing

method

Bring a pan of water to a boil and salt it well. Add the potatoes and simmer for about 15 minutes, until soft. Drain and mash, then let cool. Using a mortar and pestle, pound the garlic with the coarse salt until a smooth purée results. Add the purée to the cooled potatoes, along with the smoked mozzarella and parsley. Grind a good dose of black pepper into the mixture and stir until thoroughly combined.

Lay the puff pastry out on a cookie sheet. Spoon the potato mixture into a long, well-compacted sausage shape on one side of the pastry edge, leaving a border on that side and plenty of pastry to fold over the top of the mixture on the other side. Smooth the mixture and fold the pastry all the way around, forming a stuffed tube. Seal the ends by pressing them together. Press together the long seam, then roll the strudel over to rest with the seam underneath.

Cover and chill in the refrigerator for 30 minutes or up to 48 hours. When ready to bake, preheat the oven to 425°F. Using a sharp knife, make diagonal slashes on the top of the strudel about 3/4 in. apart and brush all over with the egg/milk glaze. Bake in the oven for 30–40 minutes, until deep golden and crispy all over. Let cool for at least 5 minutes, then slice into portions along the slashes.

sweet onion & ricotta cheesecake with cranberries & sage

This is my holiday version of Viana La Place's "Tortino di Cipolla" from *Verdura*, her brilliant book of Italian vegetable recipes. I have gussied it up with cranberries—a little vulgar maybe, but very seasonal, and a nice, tart contrast to the sweet onions. When cranberries are out of season, make it without.

ingredients

2 lb. 4 oz. fresh ricotta cheese

3 tablespoons olive oil, plus extra for greasing and drizzling

12 oz. onions (approximately 2 large), chopped

4 garlic cloves, chopped

10 fresh sage leaves, coarsely chopped

4 eggs, beaten

6 tablespoons freshly grated Parmesan cheese

salt and freshly ground black pepper

1 cup fresh or frozen cranberries

2 oz. cracker crumbs (cheese crackers or saltines),
  finely crushed

whole, fresh sage leaves, to garnish (optional)

method

Preheat the oven to 375°F. Place the ricotta in a strainer and place over a bowl or the sink. Let drain thoroughly while you cook the onions.

Heat the olive oil in a large skillet over low heat. Add the onions and cook gently, stirring frequently, until very soft but not colored. Add the garlic and sage and cook for 1–2 minutes, until fragrant.

Beat together the drained ricotta, eggs, Parmesan, salt, and pepper (ideally in a food processor) until totally smooth. Stir in the onion mixture and cranberries and mix thoroughly.

Brush an 8½ in. springform pan generously with olive oil. Sprinkle the cracker crumbs evenly over the bottom and sides, then pour in the ricotta mixture and smooth the surface with a spatula. Garnish the top with whole sage leaves and drizzle a little olive oil over the top, especially over the sage leaves. Place on a cookie sheet and bake in the preheated oven for 45 minutes to 1 hour, until firm and golden. Let cool for about 10 minutes, then transfer to a serving plate. Serve warm or cold.

think ahead

This recipe can be made up to twenty-four hours in advance. Let cool, then cover and keep in the refrigerator. If serving warm, return to room temperature before reheating.

top tip

Try to get ricotta from an Italian deli or high-quality cheese store, as it will probably be less watery and more suitable for cooking than the tubs sold in most supermarkets.

serve with

Trimmings for a roast meal

gratin of roasted garlic & squash

This is serious comfort food—a pretty outrageous dish that always pleases everyone. The squash family is huge and some members are more agreeable than others. Choose one with a dark orange, creamy, dense flesh. Butternut, kabocha, acorn, and onion squash are all good bets.

ingredients

serves 4–6

3 tablespoons extra-virgin olive oil
2 butternut squashes or other sweet-fleshed
*   squashes (approximately 4 1/2 lb.)*
8 garlic cloves
8 fresh sage leaves
9 oz. Swiss cheese, cut into 1/2 in. cubes
salt and freshly ground black pepper

method

Preheat the oven to 425°F. Chop the stem off the squash, then use a vegetable peeler or paring knife to peel off the skin. (This is much easier to do at this stage than after cooking.) Slice the squash in half lengthwise, then scoop the seeds out with a spoon and lay the squash on a cookie sheet, cavity-side up. Place two whole cloves of garlic in each cavity, along with two sage leaves. Pour about 2 teaspoons of olive oil over the garlic and sage and, using a dough brush, paint the oil all over the surface of the flesh. Bake in the preheated oven for 30–40 minutes, until tender and lightly browned around the edges. Let cool slightly.

Place the flesh in a bowl along with the roasted garlic and sage. Mash it all together with a potato masher until crushed but not entirely smooth. Stir in the Swiss cheese cubes. Spoon into a presentable, greased gratin dish and bake in the oven for 15–20 minutes, until golden and bubbly. Serve right away.

think ahead

Roast the squash one day in advance.

top tip

If you can't find a good squash, use red sweet potato. Roast whole in the skin at the same temperature, adding the garlic and sage for the last 20 minutes, lightly oiled alongside, then let cool and peel before mashing.

serve with

Roast meal accompaniments; salad; steamed green vegetables

5

desserts
little candies and naughty bites

As if you haven't spoiled your guests enough already, you can really go to town

with dessert. It's your gratifying grand finale, and no time to be judicious—everyone should feel they can dive into a dessert with reckless abandon, even if they thought they couldn't manage another bite. Dessert brings out the greedy child in all of us.

At canapé parties, some little sweet bites toward the end of the evening are a great way to inject some sugary stimulation, but can also be a signal that the party may be nearing an end. Make Baby Lemon Curd Meringues (page 96) or make the Pecan Chocolate Ripple Cheesecake (page 98) in a large, square baking dish and cut into bite-size portions.

If you're feeding a big crowd, choose Rhubarb Soup with Ginger-Studded Meringues (page 88) or one type of Eton Mess (page 87). If you're really pressed for time, they won't know what they're missing if you buy one, giant, delicious, ripe cheese—or two or three; any more and it's overkill—and some delectable savory crackers. Avoid buying lots of little pieces of different cheeses; the cheeseboard will quickly look unappetizing, and people will feel they can only take a small portion. Encourage your guests to surrender to temptation.

marrons caramelises au cognac

Chestnuts in a cognac sauce (sorry, but it just sounds so much better in French)—a quick and easy way to turn plain old ice cream into something unforgivably wicked. It's a great emergency dessert.

ingredients   serves 4–6
9 oz. whole, peeled, cooked chestnuts (sold in a vacuum pack, or in cans)
4 tablespoons salted butter
3 tablespoons sugar
^{1}/$_3$ cup cognac or brandy
chocolate ice cream, to serve

method   Carefully separate the chestnuts. Melt the butter in a skillet over moderate heat. Add the chestnuts and cook gently for 2 minutes. Sprinkle in the sugar, stir, and boil until it dissolves, about 1 minute. Pour in the cognac, stir, and turn off the heat. Let stand until just warm, then spoon over the ice cream.

think ahead   This is a last-minute recipe, but chestnuts and cognac are kitchen cupboard must-haves.

top tip   Make this as soon as the meal is finished. In the time it takes to cool off and thicken a little, your appetite should have had just enough time to come back for more. (If you have a very efficient freezer, you may want to get the ice cream out to soften as well).

serve with   Vanilla ice cream is also delicious with this treat.

tropical eton mess

Eton Mess is the absolute best dessert to feed a large, discerning crowd, as I'm sure the dinner ladies at the English boys' school know all too well—traditionally it's been served at Eton College's Founders' Day and Fourth of June celebrations. The classic version is a demure strawberry affair. Here are my two showstoppers.

ingredients

serves 8

8 individual hard-cooked meringue nests

2¹/₂ cups heavy (whipping) cream

4 tablespoons white rum (optional)

1 papaya, peeled, seeded, and chopped

1 small mango, peeled and chopped

1 baby pineapple, peeled and chopped,
    or 1 lb. 2 oz. fresh, prepared pineapple

2 ripe passion fruit

cape gooseberries, to decorate

method

Break up the meringues into bite-size pieces in a large bowl. Whip the cream until it holds its shape—do not overbeat—then stir in the rum.

Just before serving, fold the crushed meringues and whipped cream together until evenly mixed. Spoon into a serving bowl and top with the prepared fruit. Slice open the passion fruits and drizzle the juice and seeds over the top. Decorate, if desired, with cape gooseberries.

strawberry rose eton mess—Follow the recipe above, replacing the fruit with about 1 lb. 2 oz. fresh, hulled strawberries, halved if large. Instead of the rum, beat 4 tablespoons rose water through the cream. Provide extra strawberries in a bowl on the side.

rhubarb soup with ginger-studded meringues

This one is excellent for a crowd, as the portions are quite flexible and people can easily serve themselves. It looks beautiful served from a big, wide, shallow bowl, with the marshmallow-centered meringues floating on top.

ingredients

serves 10–12

4 1/2 lb. rhubarb, trimmed and sliced into 1/2 in. pieces

1 1/2 cups superfine sugar

crème fraîche or thick and creamy yogurt, to serve

for the meringues:

3 egg whites

generous 3/4 cup superfine sugar

1 teaspoon cornstarch

1/2 teaspoon vinegar

1/3 cup candied ginger, chopped

method

Place the rhubarb in a pan with the sugar and 1 3/4 cups water. Cover, bring to a boil, and simmer for 20–30 minutes, until a moderately thin compote results. Pour into a bowl, let cool, then chill thoroughly.

To make the meringues, preheat the oven to 250°F and line a large cookie sheet with parchment paper. Beat the egg whites until stiff, then beat in the sugar, a tablespoon at a time, until the mixture is very stiff and glossy. Whisk in the cornstarch, vinegar, and ginger pieces. Spoon egg-size mounds onto the cookie sheet, allowing a little space between them for expansion. Bake in the oven for 30 minutes, until crisp on the outside but still gooey in the middle. When cooled, dislodge the meringues from the paper by sliding a large knife under them.

To serve, pour the soup into a wide, shallow bowl and float the meringues on top. Serve with crème fraîche or yogurt.

kaffir lime ice cream

The splendid perfume of kaffir lime leaves gives this ice cream a subtle, fragrant undertone. I implore you, make the ice cream without kaffir lime leaves if you can't find them, as this is fantastically easy and delicious made just with lime juice or even lemon juice. You don't need an ice cream maker, just a freezer.

ingredients

serves 10–12

2¹/₂ cups heavy (whipping) cream

2¹/₂ cups whole milk

2 cups superfine sugar

6 kaffir lime leaves

²/₃ cup fresh lime juice

zest of 2 limes

method

Mix together the cream, milk, and 1 cup sugar in a large plastic container and stir until the sugar dissolves. Cover tightly and place in the freezer.

Tear the lime leaves away from their tough stems, then pound them using a mortar and pestle to release the fragrant oils. Alternatively, whack them with a rolling pin or mallet. Mix together the lime juice, zest, kaffir lime leaves, and remaining sugar in a small plastic container and stir until the sugar dissolves. Cover and place in the freezer.

Freeze both containers for about 3 hours, until slushy—the creamy mixture should be the consistency of a milk shake. Scrape the lime mixture into the cream mixture, stirring well and scraping crystals away from the edge of the container. Freeze until solid. The ice cream freezes very hard, so it's a good idea to thaw it ever so slightly in the refrigerator for about 1 hour before serving.

cranberry torte with hot toffee-brandy sauce

This incredibly luscious cake is the perfect, lighter alternative to that heavy Christmas pudding or laborious pumpkin pie. It's a pan full of sharp fruit and nuts just fused together with a little cardamom-spiked cake batter, then drenched in hot, boozy toffee.

ingredients

serves 8–10

1 lb. 2 oz. fresh or frozen cranberries

3/4 stick butter (3 oz.), melted, plus extra for greasing

1 cup superfine sugar

1 cup chopped pecans

1 egg, beaten

1/2 cup sifted all-purpose flour

1 teaspoon cardamom seeds, crushed in a mortar

3 tablespoons light brown sugar

for the sauce:

scant 1 cup dark brown sugar

1 stick butter (4 oz.)

1/2 cup heavy (whipping) cream

3 tablespoons brandy

method

Preheat the oven to 350°F. Wash the cranberries and drain well. Grease and line the bottom of a 9 1/2 in. springform cake pan with parchment paper. Place the cranberries in the pan, then sprinkle with half the superfine sugar and the pecans and mix well.

Next, make the batter. Beat the remaining superfine sugar with the egg in a bowl until well blended. Add the flour, melted butter, and cardamom, mix well, and pour evenly over the cranberries. Sprinkle the granulated sugar evenly over the top and bake in the preheated oven for 40–45 minutes. Let cool in the pan.

To make the sauce, place the sugar, butter, and cream in a pan. Stir together over a gentle heat until the sugar is dissolved and the sauce is bubbling. Remove from the heat and stir in the brandy.

Use a sharp knife or cake slicer to gently unmold the torte, letting it stand on the pan base. Slice into wedges and serve warm or cold, with warm toffee-brandy sauce.

think ahead

The torte can be made eight hours in advance. The sauce can be made up to two days in advance; cover, keep in the refrigerator, and reheat before serving.

top tip

Cranberries have a short season, but they freeze incredibly well—so stock up while they're available and use straight from the freezer in this recipe, any time of the year.

a garden party

—A relaxing and indulgent English-style tea party is a comfort zone where kids, adults, and the elderly are most at ease together. It can also be a useful context for gathering people who don't know each other too well. It's a refreshing way to make the most of sunny days: nibbling, gossiping, and celebrating for the sake of it.

The menu here is for an all-out garden party, a truly lavish affair. For a simpler version, the Cucumber & Herbed Mascarpone Bites (page 15) are essential, then choose one of the three sweet recipes. Supplement with scones (easy to bake, easier to buy) and crumpets or madeleines from a reputable bakery. Don't forget the butter, cream, and jam!

shopping
: Decorate your table. Buy flowers, lots of fruit, and plenty of sugar cubes for tea.

presentation
: If you're short on tableware, ask a friend or two to bring what cups and saucers they have, then create a funky new set by mixing cups with nonmatching saucers. Extra teapots will be a godsend.

drinks
: Not everyone likes black tea (such as Earl Grey); provide some herbal alternatives. Green tea is delicious, but it's not caffeine-free. To make the perfect pot of tea: Warm the teapot with a little boiling water and swirl; discard the water; add teabags or loose tea; then add water that is on a rolling boil. Brew it fairly strong and provide a teapot of plain hot water for those who like it weak.

the menu

broiled stuffed peaches

Good peaches can be hard to come by. Sometimes they look perfect, but have been picked unripe and taste sour and woolly. If you can, buy one from the batch and take a bite—it should be bursting with sweet juice. White peaches are often the best choice.

ingredients	serves 6	for the stuffing:
	3 ripe peaches, halved and pitted	*2 tablespoons butter, softened*
	1 tablespoon sugar	*¼ cup shelled pistachios, finely chopped*
	high-quality vanilla ice cream, to serve	*2 tablespoons sugar*
		3 tablespoons brandy
		a pinch of ground cloves
		1 tablespoon chopped candied ginger

method Preheat the broiler to its highest setting. Beat together the stuffing ingredients until smooth. Place the peach halves in an ovenproof dish. Divide the stuffing evenly between the peaches and sprinkle with the remaining sugar. Cook under the broiler for about 7–8 minutes, until the stuffing is golden and the sugar is melted. Serve with small scoops of vanilla ice cream.

think ahead This recipe can be made and assembled up to four hours in advance. Cover and chill in the refrigerator, then allow to return to room temperature before broiling.

top tip Vegans should use margarine instead of butter. Do not store peaches in the refrigerator, as their texture may deteriorate. Ready-shelled pistachios are not the easiest ingredient to find, but you don't need masses of them, so you could shell them yourself. Hulled pumpkin seeds can be substituted.

serve with Ice cream is ideal, though creamy yogurt or crème fraîche will do.

baby lemon curd meringues

Make these just bite-size for a sweet canapé or slightly larger for a light dessert. The meringues can be made up to two days in advance and kept in an airtight container in the refrigerator.

ingredients

serves 8

butter, for greasing

1–1 1/4 cups crème fraîche, sour cream,
   or softly whipped cream

2/3–3/4 cup top-quality lemon curd

pomegranate seeds, red currants, or blueberries,
   or a mixture

confectioners' sugar, for dusting

for the meringues:

6 egg whites, at room temperature

a pinch of salt

2 cups superfine sugar

2 teaspoons cornstarch

1 teaspoon vinegar

method

To make the meringue mixture, follow the recipe on page 88, adding the salt with the sugar and omitting the candied ginger. Place egg-size fluffy mounds on a lined cookie sheet, with a little room in between each. (You may wish to make them even smaller for bite-size canapés.) Flatten the tops very slightly and remember, irregularity is beautiful.

Bake the meringues in the preheated oven for 30–40 minutes, until crisp and light golden on the outside but still a little gooey in the middle. Let cool completely on the sheet. Loosen the cold meringues with a spatula and place on a tray. Top each with a spoonful of crème fraîche, sour cream, or whipped cream, and a small spoonful of lemon curd, and finish with pomegranate seeds, red currants, or blueberries. Dust with confectioners' sugar, if desired, and serve immediately.

chocolate strawberry truffle pots

These exquisite, rich little pots are ideal after a satisfying meal, when all you want is a few mouthfuls of naughty sweetness without the bulk. Make them up to eight hours in advance.

ingredients

serves 10

1 cabbage or large apple, for holding strawberries

7 oz. high-quality white chocolate

10 equal-size strawberries, hulled

10 silver dragées (candy decorations)

9 oz. high-quality semisweet chocolate

4 tablespoons butter, cubed

1 1/4 cups heavy (whipping) cream

method

Cut a slice off the bottom of the cabbage or apple to help it stand firmly, and place on a plate; this will act as a "pincushion" to hold the strawberries while the chocolate sets. Clear a space in the refrigerator that will accommodate the plate and some space above it. Melt the white chocolate in a bowl set over a pan of simmering water. Dip the pointed end of a strawberry into the melted chocolate to come halfway up the berry. Pierce a toothpick through the hulled end and then stick the other end of the cocktail stick into the "pincushion." Press a dragée into the chocolate at the very tip, if desired. Repeat with all the strawberries, then chill.

Arrange ten shot glasses or bowls on a tray, ready to be filled. Place the semisweet chocolate, butter, and cream in a pan and place over very gentle heat. Stir constantly until absolutely smooth, then remove from the heat. (If the mixture curdles from overheating, add more cream.) Divide the truffle mixture between the shot glasses or bowls, then place a chilled strawberry, with the white chocolate side pointing up, on top of the truffle mixture. Let chill for about 30 minutes, until set. Allow to return to room temperature before serving.

pecan chocolate ripple cheesecake

I created this for my mother's seventieth birthday, to be the very embodiment of delectable chocolate nuttiness, her favorite combination. She was not disappointed.

ingredients

for the shell:

7 oz. semisweet chocolate–covered graham crackers

4 tablespoons butter, melted

2 tablespoons unsweetened cocoa

for the filling:

9 oz. high-quality semisweet chocolate

2 cups cream cheese

1 1/4 cups mascarpone cheese

2 teaspoons pure vanilla extract

1 cup superfine sugar

2 organic eggs

for the candied pecan topping:

1 1/4 cups pecan halves

2 tablespoons sugar

2 oz. high-quality semisweet chocolate

method

Preheat the oven to 350°F. Crush the graham crackers in a food processor. Mix with the melted butter and cocoa, then press into the bottom of a 9½ in. springform cake pan. Pack it down firmly with your fingertips or smooth down with the back of a spoon. Bake the cracker shell in the oven for 10 minutes, then remove and let cool. Reduce the oven temperature to 325°F.

To make the filling, melt the chocolate in a bowl set over a pan of simmering water. Alternatively, melt the chocolate in the microwave. Whip the two cheeses together until smooth. Add the vanilla extract and sugar, and finally the eggs, one at a time. Pour half the mixture into the cake pan. Add the melted chocolate to the remaining mixture and stir until smooth. The chocolate mixture will be considerably thicker than the vanilla one. Spoon into the cake pan in patches over the vanilla mixture, then, using a sharp knife, swirl the two mixtures together by drawing several zigzag patterns through the mixture. Bake in the oven for 30–40 minutes, until just set. If it wobbles slightly, remember that chilling will make it set firmer.

Let the cake cool in its pan on a wire rack, then chill for at least 3 hours or overnight. Meanwhile, make the candied pecans. Place the pecans in a dry skillet over moderate heat. Sprinkle the sugar on top and stir until the nuts are toasted and the sugar becomes sticky and caramelized. Let cool.

Run a knife around the edge of the cake, then unmold, leaving the bottom of the pan attached to it, otherwise you risk breaking up the crust. Place on a large serving plate. To finish, melt the chocolate, then sprinkle the candied pecans over the top of the cake. Drizzle melted chocolate over the top to fuse the pecans in place and chill in the refrigerator until ready to serve. Allow to return to room temperature. Soak a sharp knife in hot water, dry, and use immediately for cutting each slice. Indulge.

top tip

This cake can be made as a sweet canapé. Cook in a rectangular baking pan, then chill and cut into tiny squares and separate them. Top each square with a caramelized pecan, then drizzle with chocolate.

6

at the last minute

high-speed recipes, with minimal shopping

Spontaneity delivers some of the most memorable and relaxed occasions. This

chapter is for those unexpected times in life—when old friends blaze into town without warning, when the weather is so beautiful you just have to invite some friends over after work to eat in the garden—when you can't be bothered to shop but have some hungry hangers-on to feed and you don't want them to know you can't be bothered!

Alas, a delicious last-minute meal can't be pulled out of thin air, but it can be rustled up from a well-stocked kitchen. See "The Entertainer's Bag of Tricks," page 11, and take the book with you when shopping and enjoy stocking up. If unexpected guests pop by, you can even just grab some of those tasty morsels from the cupboard and make a meal of it with some couscous and chickpeas dressed in lemon and olive oil.

Here are some superquick ideas:

Spicy soba salad Cook soba noodles, drain, and cool under cold running water. Make a dressing of sesame oil, soy sauce, chopped chilies, and scallions. Stir through the noodles and serve with lime wedges.

Cèpe cornmeal Make soft, instant cornmeal, according to the package instructions, using water in which you have first soaked a good clutch of dried cèpes for 10 minutes. (Add the cèpes too!) Stir in lots of butter and Parmesan at the end.

Fig & walnut pasta While the pasta cooks, heat some onions in olive oil until soft. Drain the pasta and stir in chopped dried figs, chopped walnuts, cubes of blue cheese, and the cooked onions.

Saffron aïoli platter Pound a garlic clove with coarse salt until smooth. Stir in 2 pinches of saffron threads soaked in 1 teaspoon of hot water, a squeeze of lemon, and 3 tablespoons of mayonnaise. Serve with potatoes and a selection of steamed vegetables.

hot & sour noodle bowl with chili oil vegan

Thick and toothsome udon noodles are available ready-cooked in vacuum packs for the quickest soups and stir-fries. They're satisfyingly slurpy in this zingy broth, but you could also use dried ramen or egg noodles, adding them to the broth early on, to cook with the vegetables.

ingredients

serves 4–6

1 lb. 2 oz. chopped, mixed vegetables from the refrigerator or freezer, such as broccoli, cabbage, cauliflower, peas, and zucchini

6 tablespoons dark soy sauce

6 tablespoons lime juice or rice vinegar, or a mixture

2 tablespoons sugar

1¼ in. piece of fresh root ginger, finely grated

14 oz. udon noodles or other cooked noodles

for the chili oil:

1 fresh red chili, coarsely chopped

1 garlic clove

½ teaspoon coarse sea salt

2 tablespoons sesame oil

method

Put 4 cups of water in a pan and bring to a boil while you make the chili oil. Pound or process the chili, garlic, and salt in a mortar or spice grinder. Whisk in the sesame oil, then set aside until required.

Add the vegetables to the pan of boiling water and return to a boil, adding the soy sauce, lime juice or vinegar, sugar, and ginger. Simmer until the vegetables are tender, then add the noodles. Cook for 1 minute or long enough to warm the noodles through.

Divide the soup between individual bowls. Drizzle the chili oil over each bowl and serve immediately.

artichoke soufflé omelette

This seriously sexy omelette will make a big impression—especially since it can be whipped up almost effortlessly. Serve with a salad or just basking in its own loveliness.

ingredients

serves 2–4

5 eggs, separated

2 whole eggs

4¹⁄₂ oz. artichoke hearts in oil, drained and sliced

¹⁄₂ cup freshly grated Parmesan cheese

10 fresh basil leaves, shredded

salt and freshly ground pepper to taste

1 tablespoon butter

2 tablespoons olive oil

method

Using a fork, lightly beat together the five egg yolks and the two whole eggs. Using a handheld electric mixer, beat the egg whites until stiff, then fold the whites carefully into the yolks, keeping it light and airy. Fold in the artichokes, Parmesan, basil, and seasoning, again being careful not to lose the fluffiness.

Heat the butter and olive oil in a wide, nonstick skillet over moderate heat. Pour in the omelette mixture and cook for about 5 minutes, until golden and crisp underneath. Depending on the size of your skillet, it may not be possible to flip the omelette with a spatula, so you can try this method: Slide the omelette onto a large plate, discard any excess oil so as not to risk getting burned, then invert the skillet over the top of the omelette and flip the plate and skillet over. Remove the plate and cook the omelette for an additional 1–2 minutes, until softly set. Slide onto a warm serving plate, cut into wedges, and eat immediately.

practically instantaneous pasta sauces

Prepared and cooked in less time than it takes to boil your pasta, these fresh sauces will knock the socks off any store-bought sauce. Don't forget that fresh pasta sauce freezes beautifully, so you can always have it on hand.

lemon spinach sauce

ingredients

serves 4

pasta of your choice

4 tablespoons olive oil

2 garlic cloves, crushed

1 small, fresh red chili, chopped, or 1/4 teaspoon dried chili flakes

10 1/2 oz. fresh or frozen leaf spinach

salt and freshly ground black pepper

6 tablespoons strained plain or thick and creamy yogurt

juice of 1/2 lemon

method

Bring a large pan of salted water to a boil. Cook pasta according to package directions or until al dente. Heat the olive oil in a wide skillet and cook the garlic and chili for 1 minute. Add the spinach leaves, season with a little salt and black pepper, and stir. Cover the skillet while the spinach wilts, about 2 minutes for fresh, 4 minutes for frozen. Take the pan off the heat and stir in the yogurt and lemon juice. Cover and let stand for 1 minute, then stir into the pasta.

fried tomatoes & hazelnut pesto

ingredients

serves 4

pasta of your choice

for the pesto:

1/2 garlic clove

1 teaspoon coarse sea salt

1 teaspoon pink peppercorns

scant 1/4 cup blanched hazelnuts

2 handfuls of fresh basil and parsley, coarsely chopped

3 tablespoons freshly grated Parmesan cheese

4 tablespoons olive oil

for the tomatoes:

2 tablespoons olive oil

2 medium tomatoes, thickly sliced

2 teaspoons balsamic vinegar

a pinch of sugar

salt and freshly ground black pepper

method

Bring a large pan of salted water to a boil. Cook pasta until al dente. Meanwhile, make the pesto. Place the garlic, coarse salt, and peppercorns in a mortar and pound to a paste. Add the nuts and pound a bit, then add the herbs and grated Parmesan. Pound and grind until a coarse paste results. Add the olive oil and stir until incorporated. While the pasta cooks, heat the oil for the tomatoes in a wide skillet over moderate heat. Add the sliced tomatoes, vinegar, and a little sugar and cook until slightly colored on both sides. Season with a little salt and pepper.

Drain your pasta, then return to the pan. Scrape all the pesto into the pasta and stir vigorously to incorporate evenly. Serve topped with fried tomatoes.

an impromptu dinner

—Here's the strategy for the menu opposite: The Kerala-Style Egg Curry (page 113) takes no more than 30 minutes to make, including preparation. So, to keep your guests nibbling happily in the meantime, prepare some delicious toasted flatbread and luxury hummus.

Turn the oven on to 400°F. Cut the flatbread into triangles and place on an oven tray. Drizzle with olive oil and sprinkle with a few sesame seeds, if you like. Toast in the oven until crisp, approximately 7–10 minutes. Scoop the hummus onto a plate; taste and stir in a little lemon juice if you think it needs it. Sprinkle with some dried mint, a few drops of olive oil, and finish with a cluster of capers. Stand some of the flatbread crisps in the hummus. Place a few pickled beets in another bowl with a few cocktail sticks.

shopping   If you do have time to shop, fresh hummus is always better than canned. Serve savory crackers in lieu of flatbread. Canned hummus is just one of the ingredients included in "The Entertainer's Bag of Tricks" (page 11), which lists useful staples to keep in the kitchen for impromptu entertaining.

presentation   At the last minute, anything goes.

drinks   If your impromptu guests come expecting to be fed, it's fair to remind them to bring a bottle of wine or a few cans of beer. Save washing up and serve beer from the can or bottle. Beer promotes good cheer, is a successful appetite curber, and tastes great with spicy food.

the menu

hummus topped with dried mint, olive oil, & capers *108*

pickled baby beets

turkish flatbread toasted with olive oil & sesame seeds *108*

kerala-style egg curry *113*

ice cream with hot toffee-brandy sauce *90*

wok-fried noodles singapore-style

It's the curry powder, pepper, and flat rice noodles that make this Singapore-style, but it's flexible, depending upon what you have in stock. Stir-fries are quick to cook, but what's the use if you're shredding, chopping, and mincing for half an hour? Preparation is kept to an absolute minimum here.

ingredients

serves 4 (more than this will be too slow and unwieldy in the wok)

5¹/₂ oz. flat rice noodles

1 lb. 2 oz. mixed vegetables—whatever you have on hand from the refrigerator or freezer; no more than 4–5 types, such as broccoli, zucchini, bell peppers, mushrooms, peas, and cabbage

2 tablespoons mild curry powder

¹/₂ cup water

2 tablespoons soy sauce

1 teaspoon salt

2 teaspoons sugar

¹/₂ teaspoon ground black pepper

¹/₂ teaspoon dried chili flakes

2 handfuls of cashew nuts (approximately ¹/₂ cup)

8 garlic cloves, peeled and left whole

4–6 tablespoons sunflower or corn oil

method

Boil a generous amount of water. Place the noodles in a bowl and pour boiling water over them. Let stand for 2 minutes—no more—then drain. Rinse under cold running water. They should be just cooked.

Cut up the vegetables so that they are in similar-size chunks. Place in a bowl and sprinkle the curry powder over them. Stir and set aside.

Mix together the water, soy sauce, salt, sugar, black pepper, and chili flakes.

Heat the wok as hot as you can—do not add oil. Toss in the cashew nuts and stir until they take on a little color, then remove from the wok. Toss in the garlic cloves (still, no oil) and char them in the dry wok, shaking occasionally, until they are blackened. Now add the oil and, very quickly, the vegetables. Stir vigorously. (Add a little more oil if it seems dry.) Stir-fry for 1–2 minutes, then add the noodles, cashew nuts, and the sauce mixture. Stir-fry for 2–3 minutes, until the vegetables are crisp and tender, the liquid is reduced, and the noodles are cooked through. Serve immediately.

think ahead

Noodles are a great quick food, so keep a selection in stock.

top tip

A traditional steel wok with a round bottom is probably the most useful pan in the kitchen if you have a gas stove. On an electric stove, you'll need a wok with a flat bottom. Large ones are best so you can really move the food around without spilling it over the sides. Traditional steel woks are thin and get very hot, which is the secret of quick wok cooking. If the wok really is searing hot, you may need a little extra oil, which is why I've given two quantities in the recipe. Always heat the wok first without oil to prevent sticking.

bulgur wheat in a spiced tomato sauce

This one is easy, fast, filling, warming, and cheap—the ideal quick-fix dinner. Inspired by an Iranian dish called *haleem*, which is a sort of thick, savory porridge, it becomes even thicker as it stands.

ingredients

serves 4

14 oz. can chopped tomatoes

1 fresh chili, sliced and seeded if large, or
   ¹/₂ teaspoon chili powder

2 plump garlic cloves

2 teaspoons ground cumin

1 teaspoon brown sugar

¹/₂ teaspoon wine vinegar

salt and freshly ground black pepper

scant 1 cup bulgur wheat

1 tablespoon dried mint

2 pieces of cinnamon stick or cassia bark (optional)

to serve:

thick and creamy yogurt

extra-virgin olive oil

a little ground cumin or cinnamon, for sprinkling

fresh parsley leaves (optional)

method

Empty the can of tomatoes into a blender and save the can. Add the chili, garlic, cumin, sugar, vinegar, salt, and black pepper and process into a smooth purée. Pour into a pan.

Pour two cans full of water into the blender in order to rinse it out, and then empty out the water into the pan. This will ensure that every last drop of purée is used. Add the bulgur wheat, dried mint, and cinnamon or cassia bark. Bring to a boil and simmer for 10–15 minutes, stirring frequently, until the bulgur is cooked. Taste for seasoning. Ladle into bowls and serve with a dollop of yogurt, a drizzling of olive oil, and a pinch or two of cumin or cinnamon on top of each bowl. Garnish with parsley leaves, if desired.

kerala-style egg curry

"Curry" is a Westernized concept meaning "stewed in sauce," and some curries are cooked to develop flavor over many hours or even days. This dazzling dish from southern India takes no more than 30 minutes to prepare.

ingredients

serves 4

4 eggs

4 tablespoons sunflower oil

2 teaspoons black mustard seeds

2 large onions, finely sliced (approximately 14 oz.)

3–4 garlic cloves, sliced

1 1/2–2 in. piece of fresh root ginger, peeled and chopped

4 fresh chilies, halved lengthwise

2 teaspoons ground turmeric

2 teaspoons cumin seeds

3 tablespoons dry, unsweetened coconut

salt and freshly ground black pepper

4 plump vine tomatoes, chopped, or 14 oz. can chopped tomatoes

1 cup yogurt

fresh cilantro leaves, to garnish (optional)

freshly cooked basmati rice, to serve

method

Place the eggs in a small pan and cover with cold water. Bring to a boil and simmer for 5 minutes. Drain, rinse under cold running water until cooled, then peel and set aside.

Heat the oil in a wok or large skillet until quite hot. Add the mustard seeds, and when they start to pop, reduce the heat slightly, add the onion, and cook until soft and golden. Add the garlic, ginger, chilies, turmeric, cumin, coconut, salt, and black pepper. Cook for a couple of minutes until fragrant, then add the tomatoes and eggs. Stir gently until heated through, then remove from the heat. Stir the yogurt into the mixture, then cover and let stand for 2 minutes. Sprinkle with whole cilantro leaves if using, and serve with the freshly cooked basmati rice.

7

fire & ice
outdoor food—picnics, barbecues, and campfires

Where there's fire, there's often ice—if you're eating outdoors. You'll be some distance

from the fridge and oven, and you'll be either warming yourself—or cooking—with fire, and icing down your drinks; or, in the case of a picnic, icing down your food. Whatever the case, food always tastes better in the fresh air.

Picnics Clever containers and cool storage are paramount. Seek out cans of all shapes and sizes to fit nonliquid foods snugly—metal stays cool longer than plastic as well as preventing squashing and leaking. Indian stainless steel "tiffin" cans and spice jars are ideal. Keep sandwich bags full of ice to wedge between your containers. A cooler with a refrigerating device, which plugs into your car's cigarette lighter, is the perfect modern picnic basket. Make a checklist—don't forget plates, napkins, cups, glasses, and a corkscrew.

Barbecues My guess is that nine out of ten vegetarians will prefer a separate barbecue grill. If you only have one, and you're cooking meat on it, borrow another or get a disposable grill. Once the coals are lit, it will take around thirty minutes before they're ready to be used for cooking. Wait until the flames have subsided; the coals should appear ashen. They should still be too hot to get close to; long-handled tongs and a long fork are essential for turning and rearranging the food.

Campfires Who said alfresco eating had to be a warm-weather affair? One of life's most exhilarating experiences is eating a hot meal by a toasty campfire in winter. Stick to one rich soup or stew, eaten out of a disposable cup with a disposable spoon, and sip mulled wine or hot cider. Discard leftovers into the fire and take your garbage home.

pressed tuscan sandwich vegan

This sandwich resembles its Tuscan sister, the famous "panzanella," a salad of bread marinated in garlic, tomato, and peppery olive oil. Here, the process of pressing squeezes these gorgeous Mediterranean flavors through the bread, which, as well as making it delicious, creates a nice, tidy package that is easy to eat on a picnic.

ingredients

serves 4

1 medium ciabatta loaf
1 garlic clove
1 medium vine tomato, chopped
10 fine black olives, stoned
2 teaspoons capers in vinegar, drained
5–6 sun-dried tomatoes in oil, drained and
   coarsely chopped
a small handful of fresh basil leaves,
   coarsely chopped
a small handful of Italian parsley leaves,
   coarsely chopped
3 tablespoons extra-virgin olive oil
1 teaspoon red wine vinegar
a pinch of salt
freshly ground black pepper

method

Slice the ciabatta in half lengthwise, then cut the garlic in half and rub all over the surface of the bread.

Place the remaining ingredients in a food processor or mortar and pulse or pound until blended to a coarse paste. Spread over one side of the bread and top with the other piece.

For the pressing, you can either tie the sandwich up with raffia or cotton string, which is very pretty, or slip it in a large plastic bag and roll up, which is easier and more practical.

Place a flat board or large book on top of the sandwich and weigh down with a heavy object—a bag of sugar, a heavy mortar, or a large container of water all work well.

Leave the sandwich to squash flat for about an hour before packing in your cooler.

think ahead

This sandwich is best made not more than four hours before eating.

top tip

Don't forget to bring a board and bread knife for slicing if taking this on a picnic. Alternatively, before departing, slice the sandwich into four pieces, then stack and tie with string or wrap in plastic wrap.

serve with

Cheese, salad

lemony lentils with radishes vegan

The cooking time of all legumes is determined by how old they are, which is the one thing they never tell you on the package. Puy lentils usually take about half an hour, so taste after that long—they should melt in the mouth without being mushy. This nutritious but delicious salad tastes great on a picnic, either packed into a well-sealed container (such as the tiffin can shown), or stuffed into a pita. It also makes a tasty side dish at a barbecue.

ingredients	serves 6–8
	2¼ cups green lentils, ideally Puy lentils
	juice of 1 large lemon
	2 tablespoons olive oil
	salt and freshly ground black pepper
	1 teaspoon fresh ground cumin
	2 scallions, sliced
	8 radishes, halved
	a handful of fresh parsley, chopped
method	Rinse the lentils in a strainer, then place in a small pan. Cover generously with water, bring to a boil, and cook at a moderate boil, without salt, until tender. Meanwhile, mix together the lemon juice, olive oil, salt, black pepper, cumin, and scallions. When the lentils are tender, drain them and mix with the dressing while still hot. Let cool completely, stirring now and then. Mix in the radishes and parsley. Ideally, it should be served at room temperature.
think ahead	This can be made one day ahead, keeping radishes separate. Stir in radishes just before serving.
top tip	Any lentil can be used in this recipe except red ones—they are too soft and lose their shape. Lentils do not have to be soaked overnight before cooking, but larger legumes, including field peas and mung beans, are safer to eat after soaking and cooking.

picnic wraps

The globalization of the tortilla has made "wraps" a popular sandwich alternative. These fillings can also be enjoyed on their own as salads: Sprinkle the chickpeas with extra parsley and paprika; omit the cream cheese from the beet.

chickpea, zucchini, & paprika wraps

ingredients

2 tablespoons olive oil
2 small zucchini, thinly sliced (approximately 5¹/2 oz.)
2 garlic cloves, chopped
2 teaspoons smoked paprika or mild chili powder
14 oz. can chickpeas
a pinch of salt
a squeeze of lemon juice
a small handful of fresh parsley, coarsely chopped
4 tablespoons yogurt
4 medium flour tortillas

method

Heat the olive oil and cook the zucchini until soft and golden. Add the garlic and, when golden and fragrant, add the paprika. When it changes color, add the chickpeas with a pinch of salt. Cook for about 2 minutes, so the chickpeas heat through and become infused with flavor, then remove from the heat. Squeeze lemon juice over them and tip into a bowl. When cooled slightly, stir in the parsley and yogurt.

Take a tortilla and place a spoonful of the filling near the bottom. Fold over the sides, then fold over the bottom and roll up tightly. Place on a plate, cover, and chill until ready to eat. Slice in half diagonally before serving.

beet, blue cheese, & walnut wraps

ingredients

3¹/2 oz. baby beets in sweet vinegar, drained and coarsely chopped
¹/2 cup walnuts, coarsely chopped
5¹/2 oz. blue cheese, such as Stilton or Roquefort, chopped or crumbled
2 heaping tablespoons cream cheese
freshly ground black pepper
1¹/2 oz. baby spinach leaves, washed and trimmed
4 medium flour tortillas

method

Combine the beets, walnuts, blue cheese, and cream cheese in a bowl. Grind in a little black pepper and mash together with the back of a spoon until evenly combined. Proceed as above for stuffing, adding a pile of spinach leaves to each wrap.

melting mushrooms

Soft, fleshy mushrooms oozing rich, dark juice and garlicky cheese—what more could you want? Serve them with bread so you can mop up every last drop that runs out of them.

ingredients

serves 4

8 large, open-cap or cremini mushrooms of roughly equal size

salt and freshly ground black pepper

4 tablespoons vermouth or white wine

2 garlic cloves, chopped

2 teaspoons fresh thyme leaves

4 oz. Swiss cheese or other melting cheese, grated

extra-virgin olive oil, for brushing

fresh crusty bread, to serve

method

Preheat the barbecue grill. Cut the stem out of the mushrooms, then score with a knife over the gills, not cutting through to the other side. Choose pairs of equal size. Lay one of each pair gill-side up on a clean counter, then season to taste with salt and black pepper. Add 1 tablespoon vermouth or white wine, followed by a little garlic and thyme, and finishing with grated cheese. Place another mushroom on top and drive a toothpick or skewer through from the top to secure together. Brush all over with olive oil.

Cook over hot coals, turning frequently and carefully, until very soft, juicy, and melting inside. Serve with crusty bread.

broiled miso-glazed eggplants vegan

If you're not familiar with miso, it's a fermented soybean paste with a strong, salty flavor. There are many types, each with different characteristics; I prefer the lighter colors to the darker ones. Miso gives a lovely depth to this glaze, which could be used for other vegetables—or anything you put on the grill.

ingredients

serves 4

large eggplant

wooden skewers, soaked for 30 minutes

for the glaze:

1 garlic clove, coarsely chopped

2 tablespoons miso

1 tablespoon tomato paste

1 tablespoon lemon or lime juice

2 teaspoons dark brown sugar

2 tablespoons sunflower or corn oil

method

Preheat the barbecue grill. Cut the eggplants into 1/2 in. thick circles and drive a presoaked wooden skewer through each piece.

To make the glaze, mix all the ingredients together in a small blender or spice grinder. Alternatively, pound the garlic with the miso paste until crushed, then whisk in the remaining ingredients until emulsified.

When the coals are hot, brush the eggplants on both sides with the glaze and cook, turning frequently with tongs and basting regularly, until very tender. Serve immediately.

broiled shiitake & tofu skewers vegan

Tofu has been around for two millennia, during which time the Japanese in particular have evolved some amazing and sophisticated recipes with the stuff. The simple teriyaki-style marinade—salty soy sauce, sweet mirin, and nutty shiitake liquor—is a long-standing winner. My "tofu mantra" is this: Keep it in its Asian home.

ingredients

serves 4

24 small, dried shiitake mushrooms
1 lb. 2 oz. fresh tofu
wooden skewers, soaked for 30 minutes
8 shallots, peeled
4 tablespoons dark soy sauce
4 tablespoons mirin (Japanese cooking wine) or sherry
sesame oil

method

Place the dried shiitake mushrooms in a bowl or large measuring pitcher and pour ⅔ cup boiling water over them. Let soften for 20 minutes, stirring now and then. Meanwhile, drain the tofu and pat dry with paper towels. Cut into sixteen chunks.

Pick out the softened mushrooms and set the liquor aside. Thread the mushrooms and tofu onto eight presoaked wooden skewers, with two pieces of tofu nestled between three mushrooms. Finish with a shallot on the end. Place the skewers in a container without stacking, so they can absorb the marinade.

Stir together the soy sauce and mirin, plus 4 tablespoons of the reserved mushroom liquor. Pour over the skewers and let marinate in the refrigerator for at least 1–2 hours. Turn the skewers over from time to time so they absorb the marinade evenly.

When ready to cook, brush the skewers with sesame oil. Cook over hot coals or on a ridged grill pan, turning over with tongs, until lightly charred on all sides.

think ahead

Skewers can be prepared up to the cooking stage one day in advance.

top tip

Don't use "silken" tofu—it won't hold together. Very fresh tofu can be bought at Asian markets and health-food stores. Try using tofu that has been frozen and thawed: It changes completely, taking on an amazing, fibrous texture.

serve with

Broiled Miso-Glazed Eggplants(page 123).

a campfire party

—An open fire brings out the pagan reveler in us. In the U.S., tailgate parties started as a gathering of football fans, beer, and fire, and have evolved into thoroughly gourmet affairs embracing the principle of enjoying the warm huddle while sharing food and drink, whatever the occasion and at any time of the year.

Before you consider hosting a party featuring an open fire, you should obtain permission and advice for building a fire; consult your local fire department. They can offer advice and guidance on where and how to construct a safe fire. Use your common sense and never abandon a lit fire.

shopping	Army surplus stores often have a good selection of camping goods that might be useful (thermoses, outdoor candles, flares, etc.).
presentation	This is one occasion for strictly disposable ware, ideally sturdy paper, which burns up in an eco-friendly fashion. Do not, however, burn polystyrene or plastic.
drinks	To make mulled wine, buy plenty of inexpensive wine. Make an infusion of one bottle of wine with cinnamon sticks, cardamom pods, and an orange stuck with cloves in a large pot. Simmer for thirty minutes, then pour in more wine and heat until hot—not boiling, or the alcohol evaporates. Fortify with brandy if desired.

the menu

parsnip & coconut soup vegan

The clever thing about this soup is that it is thick. This means it won't slosh around easily, and it stays hot while you have steamy-breathed conversations outdoors by the fire. It's rich and warming too—a meal in itself.

ingredients

serves 8–10
4 tablespoons butter (vegans: use oil)
1 large onion, chopped
3 celery sticks with leaves, chopped
1 lb. 2 oz. parsnips, coarsely chopped
10½ oz. carrots, coarsely chopped
3 plump garlic cloves, chopped
1 tablespoon plus 1 teaspoon ground cumin
salt and freshly ground black pepper
5½ oz. block of creamed coconut, chopped
4 cups strong vegetable stock
a squeeze of lemon
Corn Salsa, to serve (see below)

method

Melt the butter in a large pan, add the onion, and cook until soft and translucent. Add the celery, parsnips, carrots, garlic, and cumin and season to taste with salt and black pepper. Stir, cover, and cook over low heat, giving it an occasional stir, for about 10 minutes.

Meanwhile, place the chopped creamed coconut in a large bowl and add 2 cups boiling water. Let stand for a few minutes, then stir until dissolved. Pour the coconut milk and vegetable stock into the pan and bring to a boil. Reduce the heat to a simmer and cook until the vegetables are very soft, about 15 minutes. Let cool briefly, then process into an absolutely smooth purée. Add a squeeze of lemon juice, process again, then taste for seasoning. Serve on its own or with Corn Salsa.

corn salsa vegan—Spicy, crisp, and juicy, this is the perfect garnish for the velvety soup.

ingredients

scant ¾ cup corn kernels, blanched if fresh, or from a can, drained; ¾ in. piece of fresh red chili, seeded and finely chopped; 1 scallion, finely chopped; a few cilantro leaves, chopped; a pinch of salt; 1 teaspoon lemon juice; 1 tablespoon olive oil

method

Combine all the ingredients in a bowl and serve a small amount on top of the Parsnip & Coconut Soup.

oven-roasted hotchpotch vegan

This richly warming dish requires minimal preparation. It's one of those genuine "throw it all in the oven" kind of recipes. The choice of vegetables is entirely flexible. Mushrooms and tomatoes are good because they're juicy; the rest can be any choice of seasonal veggies up to about 2 lb. in weight. A can of beans of some sort adds flavor and protein.

ingredients

3¹/₂ oz. shiitake mushrooms
7 oz. tomatoes
9 oz. celery root
9 oz. sweet potato
2 red onions
1 red bell pepper
3¹/₂ oz. string beans
14 oz. can chickpeas, drained and rinsed
4 garlic cloves, chopped
finely grated zest of 1 lemon

a handful of chopped fresh basil and parsley
1 teaspoon coriander seeds, crushed
a good grinding of nutmeg
salt and freshly ground black pepper
cayenne pepper to taste
4 cups carrot juice, fresh or canned
to serve (optional):
thick plain yogurt
chopped fresh herbs

method

Preheat the oven to 350°F. Cut up all the vegetables into bite-size pieces and place in a deep roasting or casserole dish. Sprinkle in the rest of the ingredients and pour in the juice. Stir, then cover with foil and bake in the preheated oven for 45 minutes. Remove the foil and stir again. Reduce the oven temperature to 300°F and bake uncovered for an additional 30–40 minutes to let the juices thicken.

think ahead

Serve from the dish into warmed bowls. Garnish with a dollop of yogurt and some more chopped herbs, if desired.

top tip

Although this can be cooked in advance, there's something so appetizing about the cooking smells wafting out of the oven—it's part of the enjoyment of the dish. If guests are standing, serve the hotchpotch in mugs or cups.

serve with

Couscous, bulgur wheat, rice, quinoa, or even baked potatoes. Delicious with Mustard Garlic Bread.

mustard garlic bread—This delicious diversion from the norm is always a hit. Cook it in the oven, on the barbecue, or in the embers of the campfire.

ingredients

1 stick butter (4 oz.), softened (vegans: use margarine); 1 large garlic clove, crushed; 1 tablespoon coarse-grain mustard; freshly ground black pepper; 1 long French baguette (approximately 30 in.)

method

Preheat the oven to 400°F. Beat together the butter, garlic, mustard, and black pepper. Cut the bread into ¹/₂ in. slices, but do not slice all the way through the bottom. If it is too long to fit in the oven, cut into two pieces. Spread the butter mixture generously between each slice. Wrap the bread up tightly in foil and bake in the preheated oven for about 15–20 minutes, until thoroughly heated through and slightly crispy. Serve immediately.

8

brunch

easy dishes that taste great early in the day

Brunch, a fusion of breakfast and lunch, is, not surprisingly, an American concept,

occupying a traditional slot at Easter and on Mother's Day. Served anytime between 10:00 A.M. and noon, it can also be the party-a-day-after-the-party, usually Sunday. The hair of the dog might be required—Bloody Marys or mimosas are the order of the day.

When lots of people get together for a wedding or a big event, there is often a sequence of gatherings, culminating in a grand finale. Brunch bridges the gap between that finale and returning to normal life. It squeezes out that last bit of feasting and provides an opportunity for a relaxed winding-down from the previous night's event.

Brunch should be languorous and unfussy. No matter how few guests, brunch is a buffet—one course of many things, sweet and savory, available for refilling over and over if desired. Always provide fruit, especially melons and berries, pots of coffee, juice, and in the spirit of celebration, champagne.

turmeric potatoes with lemon & coconut

For me, crispy potatoes take the prize for the tastiest morning food. Turmeric essentially dyes these potatoes a blinding yellow while imparting a faintly earthy note in the flavor. The turmeric water turns an alarming blood red as it boils—this is OK! It's just doing its job.

ingredients

serves 6–8

2 lb. 4 oz. new potatoes, washed and halved

salt and freshly ground black pepper

2 teaspoons ground turmeric

3 tablespoons olive oil

6 garlic cloves

6 shallots, peeled

1 green bell pepper, chopped

1 lemon, thickly sliced

3 tablespoons dry, unsweetened coconut

method

Preheat the oven to 425°F. Place the potatoes in a pan, cover with plenty of water, and add a generous amount of salt and the turmeric. Bring to a boil and cook for 5 minutes. Drain thoroughly and let cool slightly. Transfer them to a roasting dish and add the olive oil. Add the remaining ingredients and toss gently with your hands, ensuring that everything is coated with a light slick of oil.

Roast in the preheated oven for about 30 minutes, stirring and dislodging sticky bits, until everything is thoroughly soft and crispy in places. Serve hot.

morning quesadillas with hot red sauce

"Quesadilla" is quite a loose term describing a Mexican-style fried tortilla encasing melted cheese, usually combined with beans, meat, or vegetables. It's usually served as a snack, but also loves the company of eggs—always yummy for breakfast. This simple, oven-baked version, though far from traditional, is handy to make in quantity.

ingredients

serves 2–4

for the hot red sauce:

14 oz. can chopped tomatoes

2 small garlic cloves, crushed

a few slices of pickled jalapeño chilies

1 tablespoon jalapeño chili juice from the jar

1–2 teaspoons mild chili powder

salt

a pinch of sugar

for each quesadilla, you will need:

about 1 tablespoon butter or olive oil, plus
  extra olive oil for brushing

1 flour tortilla

3 heaping tablespoons refried beans

2 tablespoons cream cheese

1 scallion, chopped

1 organic egg

method

Place the sauce ingredients in a small pan and bring to a boil. Simmer very gently while you cook the quesadillas.

Preheat the oven to 400°F. Spread the beans on one half of the tortilla and the cream cheese over the other half. Sprinkle with scallions and fold over. Brush generously all over with olive oil and place on a cookie sheet. Repeat with the remaining tortillas. Bake in the preheated oven for 10–15 minutes, flipping once, until golden brown and heated through.

Meanwhile, heat a little butter or olive oil in a skillet and cook the eggs to your liking. Serve the quesadillas with an egg and a little hot red sauce spooned over the top or in a dish on the side.

think ahead

The tortillas can be filled up to four hours in advance. Cover and keep in the refrigerator. The sauce can be made the day before and refrigerated.

top tip

If serving as part of a buffet, each quesadilla can be cut in half with a pizza cutter or knife to make smaller portions. Serve the hot red sauce in a separate bowl.

pine nut flatbread vegan

Flatbread makes a sassy alternative to toast. If you make the dough the night before, the pine nuts soften, forming little "stained glass" windows in the bread. Give it a whirl—it's dead simple, yet stunningly good.

ingredients

approximately 3 1/2 cups bread flour, plus extra for dusting

1/4 oz. package active dry yeast

2 teaspoons fennel seeds

2 teaspoons coriander seeds

3–4 tablespoons pine nuts

1 teaspoon salt

2 tablespoons honey (vegans: use brown sugar or malt extract)

method

Mix all the dry ingredients together in a large bowl. Dissolve the honey in 1 1/4 cups warm water, then add the water to the bowl gradually to form a soft dough. Add more flour if it's unmanageably sticky, but it should be just workable, not too stiff. Place the dough on a clean, flat counter (I use my kitchen table for breadmaking) and knead for about 5–6 minutes, until springy and elastic. Transfer to an oiled bowl and turn the dough in the oil. Cover the bowl and let stand in a warm place until doubled in size. Alternatively, place in the refrigerator and let rise slowly overnight.

Preheat the oven to 450°F. Sprinkle flour over a clean, dry counter. Gently punch the air out of the dough. Divide the dough into eight pieces and roll out with a rolling pin into flat, oval shapes. Irregular shapes are also beautiful. Place the flatbreads on a baking stone or oven tray and cook in the preheated oven for 6–8 minutes, until golden and slightly puffed. (If you have a large, flat griddle or hot plate, you can cook the bread directly on the griddle.)

whole-wheat cheese crêpes

These light and healthy crêpes require so little effort, I often make them for breakfast half-asleep, but they're good enough for entertaining, too. Tart fruit preserves are best with these, but they don't mind a little maple syrup, either.

ingredients

serves 2–4
scant ¹/₂ cup whole-wheat flour
¹/₂ teaspoon baking powder
2 teaspoons light brown sugar
¹/₂ teaspoon salt
2 eggs, beaten
heaping 1 cup cottage cheese
¹/₂–1 teaspoon butter

method

Combine all the dry ingredients in a bowl and stir in the eggs and cottage cheese. Heat a heavy skillet or grill pan until moderately hot and add the butter, swirling it around to coat the surface. Cook heaping tablespoons of batter until slightly dry and bubbly on top, then flip over and cook until golden. Serve hot with yogurt and fruit preserves.

think ahead

The batter can be made, omitting the baking powder, twelve hours in advance. Add the baking powder just before cooking. The crêpes can be cooked one hour in advance and kept warm, though they are best cooked fresh—leftover crêpes are, however, delicious reheated.

top tip

Cottage cheese usually has a plastic or foil covering under the lid—leave it in place after opening and it will keep longer.

a late morning buffet

—The morning after a long night's sleep, particularly after a long night's partying, leaves most people with cravings, either for sweet things or for a complete refueling. Eggs, potatoes, fruit, and pastries are the cornerstones of brunch. Individual espressos and cooked-to-order food have no place in this laid-back, grazing affair.

A note about eggs: The most important food to buy organic, if there had to be only one, is eggs. Compared to regular eggs, organic eggs taste much better—they have a richer, buttery yolk and a soft, creamy white. The chickens have been reared to maximize their well-being, not to maximize egg production. They are able to roam free and are fed a natural, hormone- and additive-free vegetarian diet.

shopping　　Morning gatherings will be much easier if the shopping, and much of the food preparation, has been done the day before. However, a sudden surge in numbers might warrant a trip to a bakery for some croissants or pastries.

presentation　　Warm up large dinner plates in the oven for the main dishes, and offer smaller cold plates for fruit and sweets.

drinks　　On a hot day, make iced coffee. First, brew a triple-strength pot of coffee. For those who take sugar, pour out half and sweeten with sugar while hot. Fill two pitchers with ice and pour hot, sweet coffee into one, unsweetened into another. The ice will melt and dilute the strong coffee while chilling it. Top up with milk. Make more for those who like it black.

the menu

banana, coconut, & lime muffins

Let's face it—muffins are just a crafty excuse for eating cake for breakfast. As with all good cakes, the secret is to avoid overmixing. Don't worry if there are patches of unmixed flour in the batter; they will sort themselves out.

ingredients

makes 6 large muffins or 12 small ones

$^1/_2$ stick butter (2 oz.), melted, plus extra for greasing, or $^1/_3$ cup sunflower or corn oil

scant 2 cups all-purpose flour

1 teaspoon baking powder

$^1/_4$ teaspoon fine sea salt

1 cup superfine sugar

2 eggs

grated zest and juice of 2 limes

1 teaspoon pure vanilla extract or
   1 tablespoon rum

$^1/_2$ cup yogurt

1 large, ripe banana, mashed

3 tablespoons dry, unsweetened coconut

method

Preheat the oven to 350°F and grease a muffin pan. Sift the flour, baking powder, and salt into a bowl. Beat together the remaining ingredients in a separate bowl, then fold in the flour mixture in a few swift strokes, until barely combined and still lumpy. Spoon into the greased muffin pan and bake in the preheated oven for 25–35 minutes, until golden, firm, and springy to the touch.

Let cool in the pan for 10 minutes, then turn out onto a wire rack. Eat hot with butter.

apple marzipan muffins—deliciously fruity with a knockout almond flavor.

ingredients

From the above recipe, omit the lime zest and juice, banana, and coconut and substitute: *zest and juice of 1 lemon; 1 cooking apple or large tart apple (such as Granny Smith), peeled, cored, and diced; 3$^1/_2$ oz. marzipan, cut into $^1/_4$ in. dice*

method

Proceed as for above recipe.

eggs baked in tomatoes

This idea first came to me in a dream. I made it for breakfast that morning, and it was gorgeous. A few days later, I was flicking through a newly acquired copy of Margaret Costa's *Four Seasons Cookbook*, a timeless book first published in 1970. In it, I found Margaret's Eggs Baked in Tomatoes. She recommends them as a summer appetizer, and adorns them with lashings of garlic, cream, and bread cooked in olive oil, which I'm sure could only make them even tastier if you're in that kind of mood. Still, the great collective cooking consciousness works in mysterious ways.

ingredients   serves 4, or 8 as part of a brunch buffet

8 plump vine tomatoes

4 tablespoons olive oil

salt and freshly ground black pepper

8 fresh basil leaves

8 small to medium organic eggs

4 tablespoons freshly grated Parmesan cheese

method   Preheat the oven to 400°F. Slice a tiny piece off the bottom of the tomatoes so they don't wobble, then slice off the tops of the tomatoes and scoop out the cores, being careful not to pierce the shells. Place the tomatoes on a lightly oiled cookie sheet and season the insides of the tomatoes with salt and black pepper. Lay a basil leaf inside and drizzle with olive oil. Break an egg into a cup or small glass, then carefully pour the yolk into a tomato, leaving much of the white behind (discard extra). Repeat with all the eggs. Sprinkle grated Parmesan on top and bake in the preheated oven for 15–20 minutes, until set to your liking. Serve immediately.

think ahead   The tomatoes can be hollowed out four hours in advance, wrapped in plastic wrap, and kept in the refrigerator.

top tip   If plump vine tomatoes aren't available, use beefsteak tomatoes. Cut in half equatorially, scoop out cores, and proceed with the recipe. If serving as part of a brunch buffet, place each tomato on a round of buttered baguette toast.

serve with   Buttered toast

when they eat fish

simple fish and seafood recipes for "pescetarians"

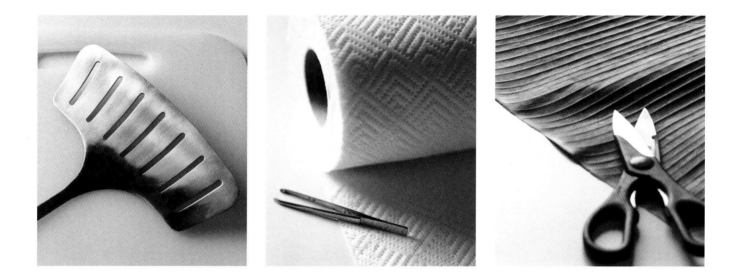

The concept of fish-eating vegetarians may seem contradictory, but the fact is, they

are a growing population. While everyone has their personal reasons for restricting their diet, the morality issues are not always the strongest. Often it's just a matter of taste.

So, this chapter is for the fish lovers!

Freshness, of course, is absolutely paramount with fish, perhaps more than any other food. Here are some guidelines on how to choose the best:

Go to a seafood store, not a supermarket—it's likely to be fresher, cheaper, and cleaner.

Don't shop for fish on Monday—it may have been caught on Saturday, or even Friday.

Ask questions. What's good today? Where's it from? If the fish merchant knows his stuff, there's plenty of interesting information to glean. Don't hesitate to ask for your fish to be completely prepared for cooking (cleaned, filleted, etc.)—that's the fish merchant's job, not yours. Save yourself the hassle. Fresh fish should look as though it's still alive and about to swim away. The eyes of the fish give a good indication of freshness. They should be clear, bright, and bulging, not cloudy or withered. Look for sparkle!

Trust your nose. If the fish smells of anything other than the sea, reject it.

For this chapter, I have selected sustainable types of fish and seafood. However, this is unlikely to apply in every corner of the world, or forever. People who are concerned about these issues must make their own educated decisions. There are many helpful Internet sites that offer information on this subject; two of the more useful ones are: The Marine Conservation Society at www.mcsuk.org and the Monterey Bay Aquarium at www.montereybayaquarium.org.

chili crab cakes with fresh sweet chili dip

Fresh is always best, but frozen crab is perfectly acceptable for this recipe, and is likely to be cheaper than fresh. Get all white meat if possible, as brown meat can taste unappealingly gamey and has a rather mealy texture. I have never been able to find crab available in any weight less than a pound, so this recipe uses it all up and makes a lot of crab cakes. Many types of crab are overfished—choose snow crab, Dungeness, or king crab.

ingredients

makes about 24, serves 8 as an appetizer
2 oz. cheese crackers or saltines, finely crushed
1 lb. 2 oz. white crabmeat, thawed if frozen,
   squeezed dry and picked through
2–3 fresh red chilies, chopped
1 tablespoon Thai fish sauce or light soy sauce
a handful of fresh cilantro, chopped
juice of 1 lime
1 plump garlic clove, chopped
1 organic egg, beaten
sunflower or corn oil, for pan-frying
lime wedges, to serve

for the dip:
1/3 cup light corn syrup
1 tablespoon light soy sauce
1 tablespoon lime juice
2 tiny scallions, finely sliced
1 large, fresh red chili, chopped, or 2 small, fresh red
   chilies, finely sliced

method

To make the dip, stir all the dip ingredients together in a bowl until thoroughly combined, then set aside.

Crush the crackers in a food processor until they are a crumbly powder. Add the remaining ingredients and pulse until evenly and thoroughly combined, but not smooth. Form into 1 1/4–1 1/2 in. wide cakes, no more than 1/2 in. thick.

Heat a shallow pool of oil in a wide skillet over moderate heat until a tiny bit of the mixture sizzles immediately. Add the crab cakes and cook until golden and crispy on both sides, then drain. Serve with lime wedges and dip.

slow-cooked fennel & squid with pink peppercorns

The general rule when cooking squid is: Cook it for under two minutes or over twenty minutes. In between is the unappetizing rubbery zone. Always get your fish merchant to clean the squid for you—unless you fancy an icky lesson in cephalopod anatomy.

ingredients

serves 4

4 tablespoons butter

2 tablespoons olive oil

1 large fennel bulb (approximately 9 oz.), trimmed
and cut from top to bottom into wedges

9 oz. squid, cleaned and cut into 1/2 in. rings

1 tablespoon pink peppercorns

salt

1/3 cup Madeira wine

2 heaping tablespoons bread crumbs

14 oz. bok choy or other leafy green
vegetable, cleaned

1 tablespoon chopped fresh Italian parsley

method

Melt the butter with the oil, which should prevent it from burning, in a large, heavy-based skillet over moderate heat. Add the fennel and squid and cook, stirring frequently, for 15 minutes.

Add the pink peppercorns, a few pinches of salt, then pour in the Madeira wine. Cook until the wine reduces, then add the bread crumbs and cook for an additional 10 minutes, stirring frequently, so the fennel and squid turn a deep golden color and the bread crumbs are cooked to a crisp. Meanwhile, put the bok choy in a steamer and cook for about 5 minutes, until tender. Just before removing the squid from the heat, stir in the parsley. Serve on a bed of bok choy with any pan juices drizzled on top.

halibut with a warm tomato & basil vinaigrette

Flatfish like sole and halibut have a supremely delicate character. This warm, barely acidic vinaigrette lends itself well to feathery-textured fish. I cooked this for a wedding party of 130 people and it was devoured in no time.

ingredients

serves 4

4 tablespoons all-purpose flour

salt and freshly ground black pepper

1 lb. 2 oz. halibut fillets, washed, left whole, or
  cut into 4 portions

2–3 tablespoons olive oil

for the vinaigrette:

4 tablespoons olive oil

4 shallots, sliced

9 oz. tomatoes, chopped

10–12 fresh basil leaves, chopped, plus extra to garnish

2 tablespoons red wine vinegar

1/2 teaspoon dark brown sugar

salt and freshly ground black pepper

method

Preheat the oven to 400°F. To make the vinaigrette. heat the olive oil in a small pan and add the shallots. Cook until soft and translucent, then add the remaining ingredients. Cook until the tomato just starts to soften, about 2 minutes. Remove from the heat and set aside.

Sprinkle the flour on a plate and mix in a little salt and black pepper, then roll each fillet in the flour mixture. Heat the olive oil in a skillet over medium-high heat. Add the fish and cook on each side until lightly colored, about 2 minutes per side, then remove the fish to a roasting pan. (If your skillet is ovenproof, place it directly in the oven.) Roast in the preheated oven for 8–10 minutes, until slightly shrunken, sizzling, and cooked through. Serve immediately with the warm vinaigrette spooned over the top and a little extra chopped basil.

a thai-style feast

—Seafood is almost unavoidable in traditional Thai cooking—hardly surprising since Thailand is made up of thousands of islands. Like most Asian cuisines, it's built around creating a heightened sense of flavor through balancing the sweet, sour, hot, and salty aspects of taste. A few exotic ingredients like tamarind, lemongrass, and kaffir lime leaves give the cuisine its unique perfume. These ingredients may be difficult to acquire, but they freeze very well, so stock up if you can.

Ornamental carved vegetables are a traditional garnish for Thai dishes on an everyday basis. Use fresh, smooth red chilies or scallions. Hold the top firmly with your thumb and index finger and slice several thin strips lengthwise. Soak the scallions or chilies in a bowl of ice water for about thirty minutes to allow them to curl.

shopping — If you can't locate a store specializing in Southeast Asian produce, investigate mail-order shops on the Internet. These recipes don't require anything too obscure—fresh chilies, limes, and mangoes should be easy to find. See notes on fish shopping at the beginning of this chapter. Note that the ice cream can be made without the kaffir lime leaves.

presentation — Thai food is traditionally eaten with forks, spoons, and fingers, not chopsticks. If you can get fresh banana leaves, they make a gorgeous lining for plates and platters. Trim to size and sterilize by pressing into a very hot, dry skillet. The leaf will turn bright green and natural waxes in the leaf will come through to a brilliant shine.

drinks — Jasmine tea is the traditional drink with food in Thailand. Fruity white wine with a bit of sweetness is a good choice.

the menu

pappardelle with scallops, saffron, & avocado

I will leave it up to you whether you want to leave the roe on the scallops—most pescetarians I've met prefer them without. This is a very subtly flavored summer dish. I first cooked it when staying in a friend's beach house; we got the scallops right off a boat from the diver himself. Strappy pappardelle carries the avocado-studded sauce nicely, but any long pasta will do. Make sure the water you cook the pasta in is as salty as the sea.

ingredients

serves 4 as a main course, 6 as an appetizer

12 scallops, cleaned and rinsed

sunflower or corn oil, for marinating

salt and freshly ground black pepper

2 tablespoons butter

4 shallots, finely chopped

1 red bell pepper, seeded and chopped into small dice

1 medium zucchini, chopped into small dice

1/4 teaspoon saffron strands, soaked in 2 teaspoons
*   hot water*

1 1/4 cups crème fraîche or sour cream

7 oz. pappardelle (long, flat pasta)

1 large, perfectly ripe avocado, chopped into chunks and
*   dressed in the juice of 1 lime*

method

Place the drained scallops in a bowl and add just enough oil to barely coat them. Season lightly with salt and black pepper and chill in the refrigerator.

Bring a large pan of well-salted water to a boil for the pasta.

Meanwhile, melt the butter in a large pan over gentle heat. Add the shallots, red bell pepper, and zucchini and cook, stirring frequently, until the shallots are soft and golden. Add the saffron water and stir in the crème fraîche or sour cream until heated through. Season with a little salt and black pepper, then remove from the heat, cover, and set aside.

Cook the pasta for about 6–8 minutes, until al dente. (Alternatively, follow the package instructions.) Heat a ridged grill pan until very hot, for cooking the scallops. When the pasta has 4 more minutes cooking time, place the scallops on the hot pan and cook for 90 seconds on each side, turning over with tongs, then remove from the heat. Drain the pasta and return to the pasta cooking pan. Stir the saffron sauce and the chopped avocado through the pasta until evenly coated. Divide the pasta between four warm plates and top with the cooked scallops. Serve immediately.

think ahead

This dish is best prepared just before eating.

top tip

Opt for diver-caught scallops, as dredging damages the seabed. Although I got my scallops from a diver, I still took them to a fish merchant to have them expertly removed from the shell.

thai tuna & mango salad

Fresh tuna is one of the meatiest fish around, and it's always a good idea to ask people how they like their tuna cooked, just like a steak. Most tuna lovers prefer it pink, as it does have a tendency to get leathery if overcooked. When selecting your fresh tuna, make sure it is labeled "dolphin friendly" and is not a bluefin tuna, which is an endangered species. Albacore tuna and yellowfin tuna are better choices, ideally if they are line-caught.

ingredients

serves 4

for the salad:

4 oz. egg noodles

1 tablespoon sunflower or corn oil

1 lb. 2 oz. fresh tuna steak, cut into cubes

1 medium mango, peeled and cut into strips

1 red bell pepper, cut into thin strips

1 small red onion, finely sliced

a large handful of fresh mint, leaves stripped

a large handful of fresh cilantro, leaves stripped

for the dressing:

1 garlic clove, finely chopped

1 fresh red chili, finely chopped

4 tablespoons light soy sauce

2 tablespoons Thai fish sauce or 2 extra tablespoons light soy sauce

4 tablespoons lime juice

2 tablespoons dark brown sugar

method

Boil the noodles for 5 minutes or cook according to package instructions. Drain, then rinse under cold water until cool. Place in a large bowl.

Whisk all the dressing ingredients together. Alternatively, mix in a blender.

Heat the oil in a nonstick skillet until very hot. Add the tuna and cook for a few seconds on each side until seared or cooked to your liking.

Pour half the dressing over the noodles and toss to coat evenly. Arrange the noodles on four plates. In the bowl that contained the noodles, combine the tuna with the rest of the salad ingredients and the remaining dressing and toss until well coated. Spoon on top of the noodles and serve.

index

for Dad

acknowledgments

My most heartfelt thanks to the dynamic team—Vanessa, Jan, and Nicky—sparks flew. Huge thanks to Stuart Cooper for keeping hold of the reins and for believing in me throughout, and to Lizzy Gray for her sharp focus and massive patience. Now for all the people who helped make this book the entity it is, with love:

Christiane Kubrick, Anya and Jonathan, Amy, Beth, and Mom, for your undying support

Suku, for auspicious friendship and the exquisite vegetable carvings, Emma, Andrew, Calum, Annette

Cathy Lowis

Tamsyn, Brent, and Shannon

Vanessa's Luke and Rosie and Mandy's Rebecca and Tilley the cat

Jennifer Joyce, Victoria Blashford-Snell

Lindsay Wilson

Recipe tasters Paula, Tracy, Ben, Kate, Paulie, Ying, Jill, Matt, Roland, Selene, James, Jessica, and little Sorrel (farther down the food chain), Rupert, Jeanne, and my lovely Dan

Rosie Kindersley and Eric Treuille and all the staff at Books for Cooks

Thanks also to: Lindy at Ceramica Blue—www.ceramicablue.co.uk; Camilla Schneideman at Divertimenti—www.divertimenti.co.uk; SCP—www.scp.co.uk; Little Book of Furniture—www.littlebookoffurniture.com; Aria—www.ariashop.co.uk; Patricia Michaelson at La Fromagerie—www.lafromagerie.co.uk; John Lewis Partnership; Renata at Giaccobazzi's; Steve Hatt fish merchants, Essex Road, London; James Elliot, Essex Road, London

Laurel Glen Publishing
An imprint of the Advantage Publishers Group
5880 Oberlin Drive, San Diego, CA 92121-4794
www.laurelglenbooks.com

First published in Great Britain in 2003 by Pavilion Books, The Chrysalis Building, Bramley Road, London, W10 6SP A member of **Chrysalis** Books plc
Text © 2003 Celia Brooks Brown   Photography © 2003 Jan Baldwin   Design © 2003 Pavilion Books

Senior Commissioning Editor: Stuart Cooper   Editor: Lizzy Gray   Art Director: Vanessa Courtier   Styling: Celia Brooks Brown   Styling Assistant: Nicki Hill

ISBN 1-59223-170-5
Library of Congress Cataloging-in-Publication Data available upon request.

Printed and bound by Imago, Singapore.
1 2 3 4 5   07 06 05 04 03